COPYRIGHT © 2007 Nanci Bell
Gander Publishing
PO Box 780
Avila Beach, CA 93424
805-541-5523 • 800-554-1819

VISUALIZING AND VERBALIZING AND V/V ARE REGISTERED TRADEMARKS OF NANCI BELL.

All rights reserved. No part of this material shall be reproduced or transmitted in any form or by any means, electronic or mechanical, including photocopying, recording, or by any information or retrieval system, without prior written permission from the Publisher. Art by Henry Santos. Printed in the U.S.A.

19 18 17 16   3 4 5 6
ISBN 0-945856-13-X 978-0-945856-13-9

SEE TIME FLY

Visualizing and Verbalizing WORKBOOK

VOLUME THREE

1610 to 1774

A Timeline of History for the Age of Kings

Nanci Bell

Hey, it's me again. Remember me? I'm Ivan—King of the Neighborhood and king of anything to do with human history. You didn't forget me, did you? Of course not. I'm not sure how I became a professor of human history. It must be that I'm so very fond of you humans.

This workbook is to help you before and after each Flight. You'll get to take a break and read words, learn new vocabulary, check your imagery with comprehension questions for the whole Flight, and write a story! I made it fun! You'll write a long story, not just a line or two, right?

Remember, you can do this. You can do anything...just like me!

Flight 1

Pre-Flight for Caravaggio

Preread words for each paragraph:

Study and visualize the vocabulary:

1
Michelangelo	local	impressed
Merisi	assistant	cardinal
celebrated	earned	Del Monte
Caravaggio	enough	offered
orphaned		

celebrated: honored by the public *(adj.)*
orphaned: deprived of parents as a child *(v.)*
talent: great skill at something *(n.)*
impressed: struck with respect or admiration *(adj.)*
cardinal: high ranking official in the Roman Catholic Church *(n.)*

Date: _____

2
honor	ordinary	use
Saint Matthew	gangly	scenes
version	repaint	figures
offended	sacred	caught
officials	beautiful	surprised

chapel: a small part of a church *(n.)*
saint: a person considered holy, moral, and good *(n.)*
ordinary: plain or common *(adj.)*
gangly: awkwardly tall and thin *(adj.)*
sacred: holy and respected by a specific religion *(adj.)*

Date: _____

3
created	realistic	instead
infamous	suffering	serene
features	scandal	beauty
models	virgin	pregnant
emotion		

infamous: well-known for bad reasons *(adj.)*
suffering: extreme pain or distress *(n.)*
scandal: a spell of mean-spirited attention and gossip *(n.)*
serene: calm, peaceful *(adj.)*

Date: _____

4
violent	Malta	managed
arrested	welcomed	seeking
brawl	thrown	refuge
island		

violent: acting with great force *(adj.)*
temper: mood, especially an angry one *(n.)*
brawl: a noisy fight *(n.)*
seeking: searching for something *(v.)*
refuge: a place safely away from danger *(n.)*

Date: _____

5
highest	few	influence
pardoned	would	Rembrandt
relieved	unique	Rubens
chasing	genius	Velazquez
collapsed		

pardoned: forgave and released from punishment *(v.)*
racked: caused great pain and sickness *(v.)*
unique: special; one-of-a-kind *(adj.)*
genius: great talent or intelligence *(n.)*
influence: to have effect on something or someone *(v.)*

Date: _____

Mark this Flight on your timeline:

← 1550 — 1600 — 1605 — 1610 — 1615 — 1620 — 1625 — 1630 — 1635 — 1640 — 1645 — 1650 — 1655 — 166

Post-Flight Debriefing

Date: _____

Flight 1: Caravaggio

Use your imagery to answer questions for the whole Flight:

A. What is the main idea for this Flight?

B. Who did Caravaggio use as models for his paintings?

 a) his friends
 b) church officials
 c) people from the streets
 d) merchants

C. Why did Caravaggio flee Rome?

 a) He was insulted by people's opinions of his paintings.
 b) He killed a man.
 c) He stole paintbrushes.
 d) all of the above

D. Why do you think Caravaggio's realistic paintings offended people?

Caravaggio had been on the run for days. He was tired and had not eaten since the previous morning. As he rounded the street corner, he...

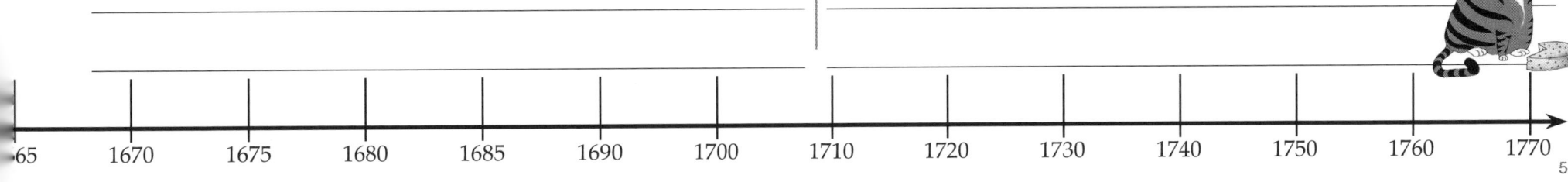

Flight 2 — Pre-Flight for Bernini

Preread words for each paragraph:

Study and visualize the vocabulary:

1
Gian, Lorenzo, Bernini, Naples, natural, sculptor, allowed, wander, fountain, plaza, statue, buildings, columns, museum, drawing

- **natural:** showing up on its own (adj.)
- **wander:** to roam from place to place without purpose (v.)
- **plaza:** an open space in a city (n.)
- **columns:** tall, decorated posts used to support buildings (n.)

Date: _____

2
devoted, bore, religious, carved, fiery, passion, anger, different, exciting, patrons

- **devoted:** gave complete attention to something (v.)
- **fiery:** intense and vivid (adj.)
- **passion:** strong feeling (n.)
- **patrons:** people who support artists and buy their works (n.)

Date: _____

3
childhood, gifted, architect, Urban, remodel, worthy, designed, colonnades, actual, tomb, founder, spiral-shaped, bronze, heavens

- **architect:** a person who designs buildings (n.)
- **worthy:** having enough value or greatness (adj.)
- **temple:** a religious building (n.)
- **founder:** one who set up or formed something new (n.)
- **tomb:** a room for a dead body (n.)

Date: _____

4
David, hero, calm, confidence, fierce, warrior, brought, twisting, tight, muscles, clenched, giant

- **felled:** knocked down and killed (v.)
- **confidence:** strong belief in one's own abilities (n.)
- **fierce:** savage and aggressive (adj.)
- **fame:** the state of being known by many people (n.)
- **sling:** to throw with a sling (v.)

Date: _____

5
ecstacy, Saint Teresa, Avila, greatest, Cornaro, awe, winged, pierce, arrow, eager, though, ability, capture, wealthy, peacefully

- **ecstasy:** great pleasure or delight (n.)
- **nun:** a woman who has devoted her life to religion (n.)
- **awe:** a feeling of wonder (n.)
- **proof:** evidence that shows something to be true or false (n.)
- **wealthy:** rich (adj.)

Date: _____

Mark this Flight on your timeline:

Post-Flight Debriefing

Date: _____

Flight 2: Bernini

Use your imagery to answer questions for the whole Flight:

A. What is the main concept of this Flight?

___

B. What city did Bernini's family move to after his birth?

   a) Paris, France
   b) Athens, Greece
   c) London, England
   d) Rome, Italy

C. What was Bernini's sculpture of David doing?

   a) slinging a rock
   b) dancing
   c) joyfully running down a street
   d) crying

D. What do you think people liked most about Bernini's sculptures?

___

Bernini took a deep breath. He lifted the large white cloth, revealing his sculpture to the crowd. They gasped and…

___

1665 1670 1675 1680 1685 1690 1700 1710 1720 1730 1740 1750 1760 1770

Flight 3 — Pre-Flight for The East India Company

Preread words for each paragraph:

Study and visualize the vocabulary:

1
Portugal, controlled, India, Asia, East Indies, Netherlands, ready, companies, united, cannons, natives, anyone, gunpoint, countries, Portuguese

- **Portugal:** a country in Western Europe between Spain and the Atlantic Ocean (n.)
- **fleet:** a group of ships (n.)
- **ports:** places where ships dock to load and unload (n.)
- **troops:** soldiers (n.)
- **dominated:** controlled or had power over something (v.)

Date: _____

2
England, queen, Elizabeth I, British, ashore, dispute, deadly, fabrics, Europe, factories, firmly

- **armed:** carrying weapons (adj.)
- **ashore:** onto the shore (adv.)
- **dispute:** a fight or disagreement (n.)

Date: _____

3
Mughal, empire, ruled, broken, chance, expand, well-trained, country, Indians, increase, profits

- **empire:** a group of countries ruled by one strong government (n.)
- **ruled:** governed; directed (v.)
- **wages:** payment to someone for working (n.)
- **increase:** to make greater or larger (v.)
- **profits:** the money gained, after all the bills have been paid (n.)

Date: _____

4
allied, angry, Robert, Clive, against, Frenchmen, deciding, Plassey, bribed, soldiers, belonged

- **allied:** joined forces in a common cause (v.)
- **deciding:** ending a conflict by having one side win (adj.)
- **bribed:** gave someone money or goods to get them to do something (v.)
- **belonged:** was owned or ruled by something (v.)

Date: _____

5
watched, monarchy, replaced, merchants, pennies, crowded, obey, education, justice, decades

- **monarchy:** a government ruled by one person, like a king or queen (n.)
- **merchants:** people who buy, sell, and trade goods; store owners (n.)
- **slums:** dirty, rundown parts of a city crowded with poor people (n.)
- **justice:** fair treatment (n.)
- **decades:** lengths of time that are ten years each (n.)

Date: _____

Mark this Flight on your timeline:

1550 — 1600 — 1605 — 1610 — 1615 — 1620 — 1625 — 1630 — 1635 — 1640 — 1645 — 1650 — 1655 — 166

8

Post-Flight Debriefing

Date: _____

Flight 3: The East India Company

Use your imagery to answer questions for the whole Flight:

A. How would you summarize this Flight?

_____

_____

_____

B. Which company controlled trade with India for the longest time?

   a) American East India Company
   b) Dutch East India Company
   c) French East India Company
   d) British East India Company

C. What happened to the Native Indians once the British took control?

   a) They became wealthy from their high earnings.
   b) They grew poorer and lived in dirty slums.
   c) They went to school.
   d) They built more Indian factories, which were controlled by the Indian government.

D. Why do you think the British treated the Indians so poorly?

_____

_____

British soldiers stormed into the store, sending jars full of pepper crashing to the floor. The Indian man who owned store yelled…

_____

_____

_____

_____

_____

_____

_____

_____

_____

_____

_____

_____

_____

_____

_____

_____

Flight 4 — Pre-Flight for Dutch Golden Age

Preread words for each paragraph:

Study and visualize the vocabulary:

1
huge	Germany	foreign
growing	loaded	farther
either	leaky	dollar
nestled	studied	

crops: plants grown for food or sale (n.)
leaky: letting water in or out by accident (adj.)
foreign: from outside one's own country (adj.)

Date: _____

2
improving	Philip II	prince
Charles I	taxes	Orange
jealous	thriving	rebelled
Spanish	looting	fought
stealing	burning	freedom

jealous: wanting something that someone else has (adj.)
taxes: fees paid to the government (n.)
thriving: living well and increasing in number (v.)
looting: stealing goods by force (v.)
rebelled: fought against someone in control (v.)

Date: _____

3
fighting	strength	tons
tripled	Amsterdam	richest
carry	crammed	

tripled: made three times larger (v.)
crammed: many things forced into a small space (v.)
bound: going; on the way (adj.)

Date: _____

4
sailor	discovered	inland
Henry	claimed	Manhattan
Hudson	timber	confident
route	tobacco	protect

route: a path that one travels (n.)
claimed: took control of (v.)
timber: wood used for building (n.)

Date: _____

5
strongest	defenseless	undefended
busy	colony	splinters
profitable	easily	golden
seize	joined	age

seize: to take control of something by force (v.)
defenseless: having no protection (adj.)
colony: settlement of people who moved to a land ruled by their home country (n.)
splinters: small thin pieces of wood broken off a larger piece (n.)

Date: _____

Mark this Flight on your timeline:

1550　1600　1605　1610　1615　1620　1625　1630　1635　1640　1645　1650　1655　1660

Post-Flight Debriefing

Date: _____

Flight 4: Dutch Golden Age

Use your imagery to answer questions for the whole Flight:

A. What is this Flight about?

_____

_____

_____

B. What city became the richest port in the world in the 1600's?

   a) New York
   b) Hamburg
   c) Amsterdam
   d) Hong Kong

C. What country had a fleet of ships strong enough to match the Dutch?

   a) France
   b) England
   c) Spain
   d) Japan

D. Why do you think this time is called the Dutch Golden Age?

_____

_____

_____

At the Manhattan Island port, Dutch traders loaded their ship with goods. Suddenly the lookout cried that English ships were on the horizon. The traders…

_____

_____

_____

_____

_____

_____

_____

_____

_____

_____

_____

_____

_____

_____

Flight 5

Pre-Flight for The First Americans

Preread words for each paragraph:

Study and visualize the vocabulary:

1
- America
- crossed
- frigid
- weather
- buffalo
- developed
- completely
- languages
- lifestyles
- nomads
- wanderers
- villages
- assuring

frigid: extremely cold (adj.)
herds: groups of animals (n.)
nomads: people who often move from place to place (n.)
assuring: causing to be sure of having something (v.)
paved: covered with stones, bricks, tiles, or concrete, to make hard and flat (v.)

Date: _____

2
- Aztec
- Incan
- European
- conquered
- Mexico
- worshiped
- kingdoms
- spread
- Andes
- terraces
- priests
- Cuzco
- calendars
- movement
- harvest

conquered: took over control by force (v.)
worshiped: paid honor and respect to something (v.)
kingdoms: the lands and people ruled by a king or queen (n.)
terraces: flat ledges on the side of a hilly slope (n.)

Date: _____

3
- nomadic
- Apache
- Sioux
- followed
- roaming
- gathering
- berries
- thatched
- teepees
- quickly
- Cherokee
- Iroquois
- squash
- bear
- solid

thatched: made of straw or leaves (adj.)
teepees: cone-shaped tents made of animal skins, built by Native Americans (n.)
wigwam: a dome-shaped hut made of grass and wood, built by Native Americans (n.)
longhouse: long, narrow, one-room homes built by some Native Americans (n.)
shingles: thin, flat pieces of wood used to cover roofs (n.)

Date: _____

4
- wigwams
- longhouses
- roofed
- shingles
- rainwater
- Christopher
- Columbus
- mistake
- discovery
- stolen
- nearly
- customs
- cultures

stolen: taken from someone without permission (v.)
stake: to make or set apart, especially a claim (v.)
customs: practices or habits (n.)
cultures: ways of life for certain people or countries (n.)

Date: _____

5
- centuries
- sandy
- changed
- stormed
- jewels
- armor
- helmets
- armies
- settlers
- Plymouth
- Jamestown
- survived
- unhappy
- further

centuries: lengths of time, one hundred years each (n.)
jewels: precious stones like diamonds, rubies, and emeralds (n.)
armor: metal plates worn for protection (n.)
settlers: people who move to a new country to live (n.)

Date: _____

Mark this Flight on your timeline:

1550 — 1600 — 1605 — 1610 — 1615 — 1620 — 1625 — 1630 — 1635 — 1640 — 1645 — 1650 — 1655 — 1660

Post-Flight Debriefing

Date: _____

Flight 5: The First Americans

Use your imagery to answer questions for the whole Flight:

A. What is the main idea for this Flight?

_____
_____
_____

B. Where did the Aztec tribe live?

    a) Mexico
    b) Brazil
    c) Oregon
    d) Florida

C. Why were the Spanish able to conquer the native Aztec and Incan empires?

    a) The native armies were too small.
    b) The natives ran out of gold and had nothing left to trade with the Spanish.
    c) The natives did not know how to fight.
    d) The natives had no armor to protect them from Spanish guns.

D. How do you think the Native Americans felt about the arrival of people from Europe?

_____
_____
_____

Columbus and his men rowed toward the beach. He saw natives walk out of the jungle, watching him. As his boat reached the shore…

_____
_____
_____
_____
_____
_____
_____
_____
_____
_____
_____
_____
_____

Flight 6

Pre-Flight for Pocahontas & Jamestown

Preread words for each paragraph:

Study and visualize the vocabulary:

1
gold-seekers, Atlantic, dropped, northern
Powhatan, strange, injuring
wooden, disease, hunger

anchor: a hooked metal weight that secures ships from drifting off (n.)
raid: a surprise attack (n.)
hunger: a strong need for food (n.)

Date: _____

2
endless, bitter, captain, scared, digging
risked, ambushed, chief, stretched, heavy
begging, mercy, spared, friend

bitter: painful; unpleasant (adj.)
ambushed: attacked by surprise (v.)
mercy: forgiveness or kindness toward an enemy (n.)
spared: held back from hurting or killing someone (v.)

Date: _____

3
Pocahontas, daughter, blankets, iron
visited, instrument, preserve, famine
utter, confusion, worse

harsh: rough; severe; hard to survive (adj.)
instrument: a person who helped do something (n.)
preserve: protect from harm; maintain (v.)
famine: an extreme lack of food, causing sickness and death (n.)
confusion: disorder and chaos (n.)

Date: _____

4
leader, kidnapped, docked
starving, mistreated, beliefs
Rolfe, married, uneasy

kidnapped: took a person away by force (v.)
docked: tied to a dock (v.)
starving: seriously lacking enough food to eat (adj.)
mistreated: treated poorly; tortured or punished (v.)

Date: _____

5
husband, honored
deathly, carried
survival

honored: praised and respected (v.)
damp: slightly wet (adj.)
ill: sick (adj.)

Date: _____

Mark this Flight on your timeline:

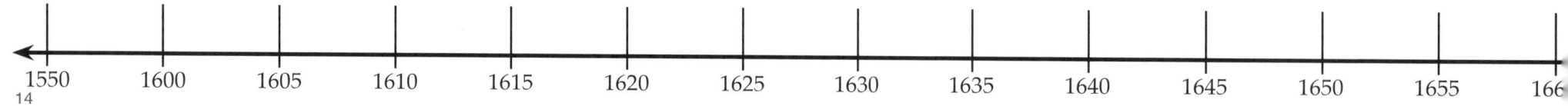

Post-Flight Debriefing

Date: _____

Flight 6: Pocahontas & Jamestown

Use your imagery to answer questions for the whole Flight:

A. What is the main concept of this Flight?

_____

_____

_____

B. What did the Powhatan tribe trade their corn and blankets for?

  a) freshly grown oranges and bananas
  b) silk and cotton fabrics
  c) copper pots and iron tools
  d) diamond jewelry

C. Where did the Jamestown colony leader keep Pocahontas while she was kidnapped?

  a) on a ship docked in the bay
  b) tied to a tree deep in the forest
  c) in a cave along the coast
  d) none of the above

D. Why do you think Pocahontas helped John Smith and his colony?

Smith and his men heard a loud scream from behind the trees. Arrows flew past their heads. Smith tried to run but…

_____

_____

_____

_____

_____

_____

_____

_____

_____

_____

_____

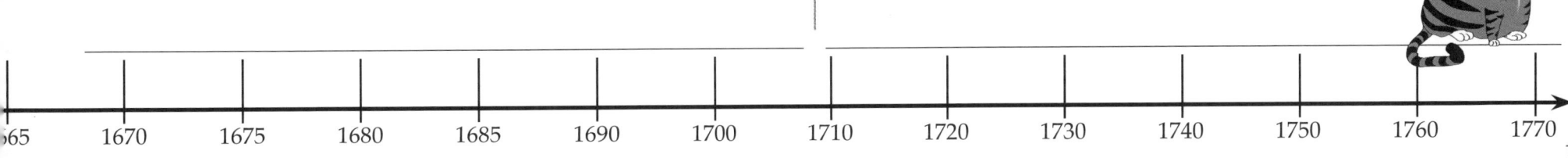

Flight 7

Pre-Flight for The Baroque Period

Preread words for each paragraph:

Study and visualize the vocabulary:

1.
boring	finest	splendor
Lutheran	materials	Baroque
glory	murals	period
colorful	choirs	droves
cathedrals	inspired	excited

Date: _____

pomp: impressive appearance or show (*n.*)
cathedrals: very large and important churches, often built of stone (*n.*)
murals: large paintings on the wall of a building (*n.*)
choirs: groups of people who sing (*n.*)
droves: large crowds of people (*n.*)

2.
gasp	shadow	alive
vivid	drama	superheroes
powerful	subjects	human
crisis	Bible	

Date: _____

gasp: a deep, quick breath, usually taken in shock (*n.*)
vivid: bright and full of life (*adj.*)
crisis: a time of extreme conflict or danger (*n.*)
myth: an ancient, well-known story (*n.*)

3.
fancy	grandest	skillfully
arches	Louis XIV	invisible
ornate	Versailles	intricate
gardens	mirrors	ceilings
palaces	portraits	furniture

Date: _____

ornate: decorated (*adj.*)
palaces: large houses for royalty (*n.*)
portraits: paintings of a person (*n.*)
intricate: detailed and complex (*adj.*)

4.
dramatic	melody	nobles
composers	audiences	royals
harmony	operas	competed
counterpoint	majesty	guests

Date: _____

composers: people who write music (*n.*)
harmony: the use of musical notes that sound pleasing together (*n.*)
operas: plays in which the actors sing their lines instead of speaking them (*n.*)
majesty: impressiveness and beauty (*adj.*)

5.
hairstyles	powder	lavish
fancier	makeup	costumes
towering	masquerade	wealth
dyed		

Date: _____

satin: a smooth, shiny fabric made of silk (*n.*)
masquerade ball: a party in which the guests wear costumes and masks (*n.*)
lavish: a very large amount of something (*adj.*)

Mark this Flight on your timeline:

1550 | 1600 | 1605 | 1610 | 1615 | 1620 | 1625 | 1630 | 1635 | 1640 | 1645 | 1650 | 1655 | 166

Post-Flight Debriefing

Date: _____

Flight 7: The Baroque Period

Use your imagery to answer questions for the whole Flight:

A. How would you summarize this Flight?

Based on your imagery, write a Picture Summary for this Flight.

B. How did churches get people to start going to services again?

  a) They gave people money to go to church.
  b) They gave out free food during the service.
  c) They sent people to jail if they did not attend church.
  d) They filled the churches with artwork and the choirs sang new music.

C. What was considered to be the grandest palace built during the Baroque Period?

  a) the White House
  b) the Parthenon in Greece
  c) Buckingham Palace in England
  d) the Palace of Versailles in France

D. Do you think the people of Europe enjoyed church during the Baroque Period? Why or why not?

1665 1670 1675 1680 1685 1690 1700 1710 1720 1730 1740 1750 1760 1770

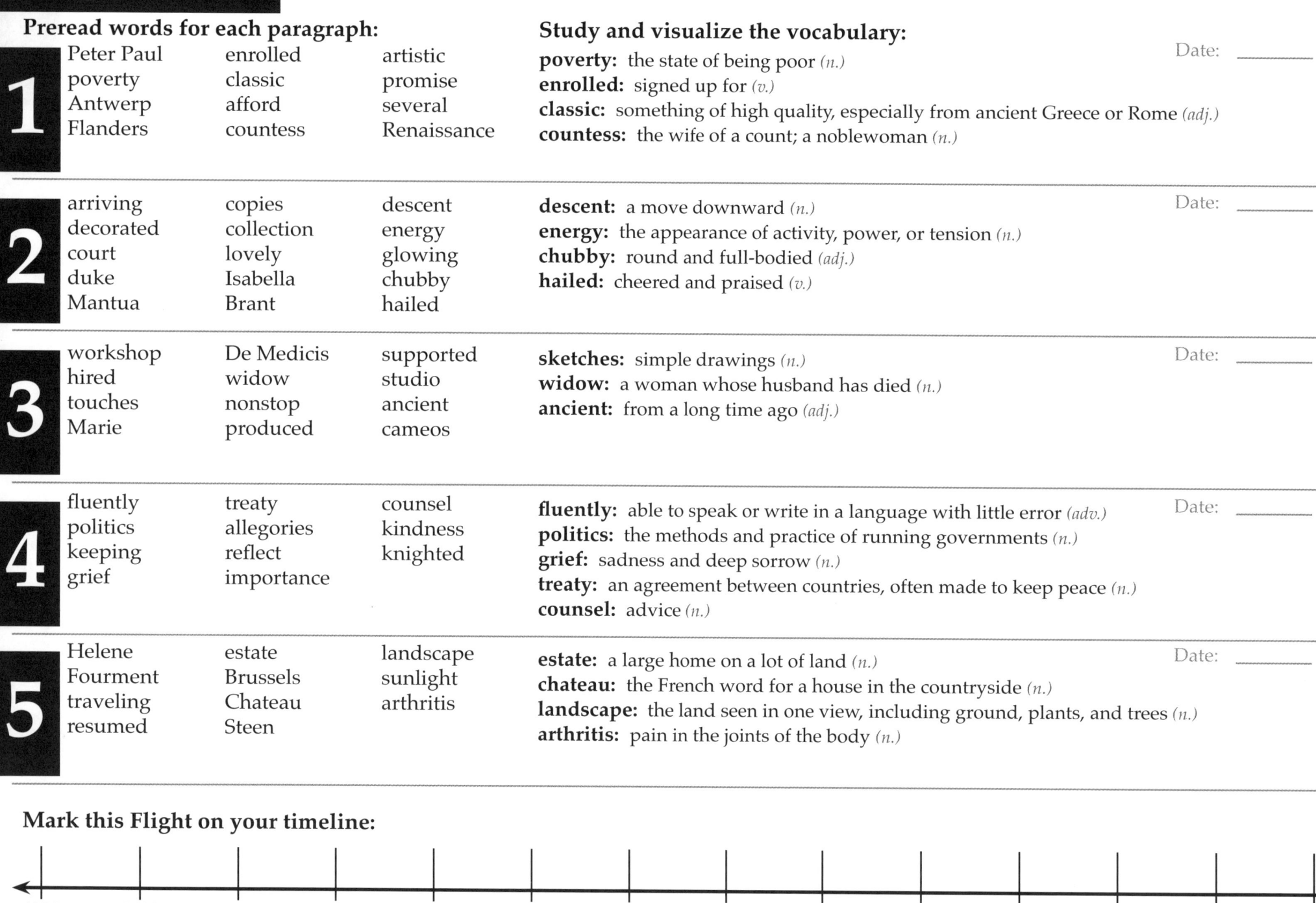

Post-Flight Debriefing

Date: _____

Flight 8: Peter Paul Rubens

Use your imagery to answer questions for the whole Flight:

A. What is this Flight about?

_____

_____

_____

B. Why did Rubens feel the need to go to Italy?

  a) He was bored in Antwerp and wanted a change.
  b) Italy is where all the great painters of the Renaissance lived.
  c) The painters in Antwerp were not good enough to teach Rubens anything.
  d) Italy had more art schools for Rubens to attend.

C. What did the 21 paintings for Marie de Medicis depict?

  a) her life story
  b) her pets
  c) her late husband, the King of France
  d) her dreams

D. How did Rubens' artwork help make peace between England and Spain?

_____

_____

_____

Rubens's hands ached, but he continued painting. It was nearly sunrise, and he was almost finished. A sudden knock at the door startled him. He…

_____

_____

_____

_____

_____

_____

_____

_____

_____

_____

_____

_____

_____

_____

_____

_____

_____

1665 1670 1675 1680 1685 1690 1700 1710 1720 1730 1740 1750 1760 1770

Flight 9 — Pre-Flight for Baroque Painters

Preread words for each paragraph:

Study and visualize the vocabulary:

Date: _____

1
Diego	Seville	capital
wealthiest	Madrid	grotesque
deformed		

deformed: odd or ugly in shape (*adj.*)
grotesque: ugly and strange looking (*adj.*)

Date: _____

2
unusual	viewer	servants
Las Meninas	couple	surround
princesses	reflection	cleverness
posed		

dwarf: a person who is smaller than most people (*n.*)
posed: sat or stood still in order to be painted (*v.*)
servants: people who work for the rich, helping with their home or land (*n.*)
raved: praised and spoke highly of something (*v.*)
cleverness: quick thinking; intelligence (*n.*)

Date: _____

3
Flemish	elegant	realism
Anthony	slender	posers
Van Dyck	midst	lovelier
perfected	tapestries	

elegant: graceful and beautiful (*adj.*)
slender: thin (*adj.*)
midst: in the middle of something (*n.*)
tapestries: an artwork of woven fabric, often hung on a wall (*n.*)
realism: the state of looking the way things look in real life (*n.*)

Date: _____

4
satin	touched	vain
shimmer	personal	pompous
velvet	hunting	regal

shimmer: to shine lightly (*v.*)
velvet: a thick, soft fabric (*n.*)
vain: thinking highly of one's own appearance (*adj.*)
pompous: thinking too highly of one's self (*adj.*)
regal: royal and important, as of a king or queen (*adj.*)

Date: _____

5
Jan	tasks	admired
Vermeer	sewing	innkeeper
photographs	shining	achieve
simple		

panes: the glass sections of a window (*n.*)
admired: well-liked and respected (*v.*)
innkeeper: a person who runs an inn or hotel (*n.*)

Mark this Flight on your timeline:

Post-Flight Debriefing

Date: _____

Flight 9: Baroque Painters

Use your imagery to answer questions for the whole Flight:

A. What is the main idea for this Flight?

_____

_____

_____

B. Who hired Van Dyck to be his personal painter?

    a) Czar Michael Romanov of Russia
    b) Queen Elizabeth I of England
    c) King Louis XIII of France
    d) King Charles I of England

C. What did Dutch artist Jan Vermeer like to paint?

    a) kings and queens
    b) the hills and rivers of Holland
    c) girls who are sewing, cooking, reading, or eating
    d) his wife and 11 kids

D. Why do you think the paintings of Velazquez, Van Dyck, and Vermeer became so famous?

_____

_____

_____

Write a Word Summary for this Flight.

1665 | 1670 | 1675 | 1680 | 1685 | 1690 | 1700 | 1710 | 1720 | 1730 | 1740 | 1750 | 1760 | 1770

Flight 10 — Pre-Flight for The Pilgrims

Preread words for each paragraph:

Study and visualize the vocabulary:

1
Puritans, stoic, craftsmen
believed, persecution, expensive
strongly

stoic: seeming not to be bothered by pain or suffering *(adj.)*
persecution: the cruel treatment of people, often done for religious reasons *(n.)*
craftsmen: people who are skilled at making things *(n.)*
odds: a state of disagreement or dislike *(n.)*

Date: _____

2
anymore, low-paying, argued
furious, disliked, Holland
Pilgrims

furious: very mad *(adj.)*
argued: gave reasons for and against something *(v.)*

Date: _____

3
raised, stuffy, Mayflower
Speedwell, smelly, compact
rough, grumpy, agreement
seasick, sighted, wiser
sway, weary

funds: money for a certain purpose *(n.)*
sway: the rocking back and forth of something *(n.)*
weary: tired *(adj.)*

Date: _____

4
searched, sickness, fringed
founded, survivors, loinskin
plantation, already, arrived
families, Samoset, stunned

founded: set up or started something *(v.)*
plantation: a new settlement *(n.)*
fringed: having strings or strips of material hanging from the edge, usually on fabric *(adj.)*
loinskin: a piece of animal skin that is worn wrapped around the hips *(n.)*

Date: _____

5
Squanto, feast, worst
pumpkins, invited, luckily
turkeys, dangerously, larger
harvested

local: being from a particular place *(adj.)*
harvested: gathered crops to eat or store *(v.)*
feast: a large meal, often held to celebrate something *(n.)*

Date: _____

Mark this Flight on your timeline:

1550 1600 1605 1610 1615 1620 1625 1630 1635 1640 1645 1650 1655 166

Post-Flight Debriefing

Date: _____

Flight 10: The Pilgrims

Use your imagery to answer questions for the whole Flight:

A. What is the main concept of this Flight?

_____

_____

_____

B. Why did the Pilgrims only use the *Mayflower* to sail to the New World and not the *Speedwell* too?

    a) The *Speedwell* was needed by Holland for their war with Spain.
    b) The *Mayflower* was a larger ship and could hold everyone easily.
    c) The *Speedwell* had leaks.
    d) none of the above

C. Why did the Pilgrims celebrate *Thanksgiving*?

    a) They were happy to have escaped English persecution.
    b) They had grown and gathered an excess of food for the winter.
    c) It was a native tradition they learned from Samoset and Squanto.
    d) They had just survived winter and wanted to celebrate the spring.

D. What do you think would have happened to the Pilgrims if they had not met Samoset and Squanto?

_____

_____

The Pilgrims huddled together to keep warm. They had been on the ocean for two months and longed to set foot on land. Suddenly the boat rocked violently and…

_____

_____

_____

_____

_____

_____

_____

_____

_____

_____

_____

_____

_____

_____

_____

Flight 11

Pre-Flight for Rembrandt

Preread words for each paragraph:

Study and visualize the vocabulary:

1
- Van Rijn
- supposed
- become
- doctor
- planned
- future
- Pieter
- Lastman
- surpassed
- flocked

capital: the city where the government rules from (adj.)
surpassed: went beyond (v.)
flocked: came in large groups (v.)

Date: _____

2
- bathed
- anatomy
- Dr.
- Nicholaes
- Tulp
- commissioned
- snapshots
- medical
- huddled
- listen
- lecture
- dissects
- gathered
- expression
- originality

commissioned: asked and paid for something to be done (v.)
anatomy: the study of a living body (n.)
pale: having little color (adj.)
expression: the look on someone's face that shows mood (n.)
originality: the state of being new and creative (n.)

Date: _____

3
- often
- pearls
- happiness
- Titus
- adored
- tragedy
- Saskia
- ill-fated
- sadness

adored: loved very much (v.)
tragedy: a bad and unfortunate event that causes great pain (n.)
ill-fated: certain to have bad luck (adj.)

Date: _____

4
- guards
- shadowy
- single
- officer
- uniform
- everyone
- moving
- scene
- canvas

officer: a police or military leader (n.)
sash: a long, thin piece of fabric, worn draped across the chest or tied around the waist (n.)
peers: looks out (v.)
canvas: rough fabric, often used to paint on (n.)

Date: _____

5
- spending
- debts
- beloved
- etchings
- weapons
- applied
- succumbed
- plague

debts: money owed to someone (n.)
etchings: drawings scratched into metal plates (n.)
succumbed: gave in; died from (v.)
plague: a deadly disease that killed thousands of people across Europe (n.)

Date: _____

Mark this Flight on your timeline:

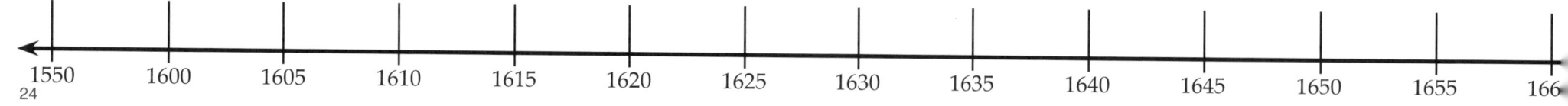

1550 1600 1605 1610 1615 1620 1625 1630 1635 1640 1645 1650 1655 166

Post-Flight Debriefing

Date: _____

Use your imagery to answer questions for the whole Flight:

A. How would you summarize this Flight?

B. What did Rembrandt's father want Rembrandt to become?

   a) a sailor
   b) a doctor
   c) a painter
   d) a writer

C. What scene did Rembrandt paint in his *Anatomy Lesson of Dr. Nicholaes Tulp*?

   a) children playing in a lake
   b) angels overlooking a newborn child
   c) the death of his wife, Saskia
   d) students watching a doctor dissect a dead body

D. How do you think the events in Rembrandt's life affected his paintings?

The students gathered around the doctor as Rembrandt set up his paints and canvas. Then as the doctor began to lift the sheet off the body…

Flight 11: Rembrandt

Flight 12

Pre-Flight for Christina of Sweden

Preread words for each paragraph:

Study and visualize the vocabulary:

1
Christina, Maria, thirty
Sweden, Eleanora, regents
Gustavus, disappointment, despite
Adolphus, deceived, princely
predicted, private, continued

predicted: told of beforehand (v.)
disappoinment: something that makes one feel let down (n.)
private: for only one person (adj.)
tutors: people who teach one student at a time (n.)
Regents: people who rule in place of a king or queen who is too young (n.)

Date: _____

2
dying, strong-willed, Westphalia
advisors, diplomat

struggle: a fight or conflict (n.)
advisors: people who give advice (n.)
diplomat: a person working for one country who talks to other countries (n.)
draft: to write a rough plan (v.)

Date: _____

3
curious, convert, crown
amassed, outlawed, thinker
library, refused, cousin
Catholic, divine, unknown

curious: interested and eager to learn (adj.)
amassed: gathered or collected for one's self (v.)
convert: to change from one thing to another, especially with religions (v.)
outlawed: ruled out; banned (v.)
divine: coming from God or a god (adj.)

Date: _____

4
unanswered, urge, prepare
questions, nearby, regain
sudden, province

urge: a strong desire to do something (n.)
province: a part or division of a country (n.)
rage: anger or fury (n.)

Date: _____

5
literature, public, apologies
maxims, Academia Reale
theater

literature: books and writings that are considered great (n.)
drama: the art of writing or showing plays (n.)
maxims: short statements about ideas or ways of behaving (n.)
theater: a place where plays and music are performed (n.)
apologies: statements that one is sorry for doing something wrong (n.)

Date: _____

Mark this Flight on your timeline:

1550 1600 1605 1610 1615 1620 1625 1630 1635 1640 1645 1650 1655 1660

Post-Flight Debriefing

Date: _____

Flight 12: Christina of Sweden

Use your imagery to answer questions for the whole Flight:

A. What is this Flight about?

_____

_____

_____

B. Why did Christina give up her Swedish throne?

  a) She did not get along with her advisors.
  b) She wanted to study a religion that was outlawed in Sweden.
  c) The people of Sweden no longer wanted to be ruled by a woman.
  d) all of the above

C. What happened to the man who betrayed Christina's plans to take control of Sweden once again?

  a) Christina killed him.
  b) He fled Naples and was never seen again.
  c) He apologized and they made new plans to take control of Sweden.
  d) He formed his own army and tried to fight Christina's soldiers for the Swedish throne.

D. Do you think it was a good idea for Christina's father to raise her as a boy? Why or why not?

_____

_____

Christina walked down a dark alley. A priest greeted her and led her through a secret door. Suddenly they heard a scuffle outside, and Christina…

_____

_____

_____

_____

_____

_____

_____

_____

_____

_____

_____

_____

_____

_____

Flight 13

Pre-Flight for René Descartes

Preread words for each paragraph:

1
René	Jesuit	written
Descartes	sickly	translated
politician	discharge	challenge

Study and visualize the vocabulary:

Jesuit: a division of the Catholic religion that trains priests *(adj.)*
discharge: release from service *(n.)*
translated: changed from one language to another *(v.)*
challenge: a hard task *(n.)*

Date: _____

2
college	lifelong	knowledge
solve	studying	dedicate
problem	spirit	scientists
promptly	truth	scholars
correct	treasures	

promptly: done quickly *(adv.)*
knowledge: learned facts and ideas *(n.)*
scholars: people who have learned much about something *(n.)*

Date: _____

3
selfish	Principia	patience
preferred	Philosophiae	pension
whispers	thirst	regular
Meditationes		

cold: with little or no emotion *(adj.)*
selfish: thinking only of oneself *(adj.)*
patience: the ability to wait calmly without complaining *(n.)*
company: people gathered around one *(n.)*

Date: _____

4
pictured	morning	attention
physics	constant	secluded
philosophy	lunches	frequently
medicine		

physics: the study of matter and energy and how the two relate *(n.)*
philosophy: the study of thought and of the meaning of life *(n.)*
secluded: away from others; out of sight *(adj.)*
frequently: often; occurring many times *(adv.)*

Date: _____

5
attempts	Bohemia	tutored
avoid	particularly	ambitious
elusive	exchanged	arrogant
sought		

elusive: hard to find or make contact with *(adj.)*
particularly: especially; to a great degree *(adj.)*
ambitious: eager to gain something, such as wealth, power, or knowledge *(adj.)*
frail: weak and fragile *(adj.)*
arrogant: overly proud and pushy *(adj.)*

Date: _____

Mark this Flight on your timeline:

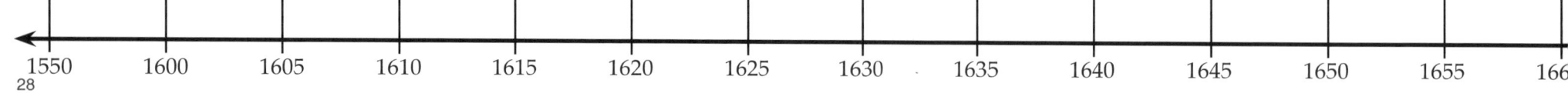

Post-Flight Debriefing

Date: _____

Flight 13: Rene Descartes

Use your imagery to answer questions for the whole Flight:

A. What is the main idea for this Flight?

_____
_____
_____

B. What was written on the Dutch sign?

    a) directions to the next town
    b) a difficult math challenge
    c) an advertisement for the local food market
    d) a flyer for a missing dog

C. How did Descartes picture knowledge?

    a) like a sailboat sailing to the New World through stormy seas
    b) like a child as he grows into a man
    c) like a house with its doors, windows, roof, and everything inside
    d) like a tree with its thick trunk, roots, and branches

D. Why do you think Descartes preferred to live a quiet life, alone?

_____
_____
_____

Descartes walked through the grand entrance of the castle and into the ballroom. Guests swarmed to greet him. He…

_____
_____
_____
_____
_____
_____
_____
_____
_____
_____
_____
_____
_____

Flight 14

Pre-Flight for Charles & Cromwell

Preread words for each paragraph:

Study and visualize the vocabulary:

1
stammering, spoiled, executed, reign, above, whatever, apply, Parliament, disagreed, members, defied, enemies, civil

- **stammering:** speaking with many sudden pauses and repeated sounds (*adj.*)
- **spoiled:** having bad character from being given too much (*adj.*)
- **executed:** killed by order of the law (*v.*)
- **reign:** a king or queen's time of rule (*n.*)
- **defied:** went against someone or something; disobeyed (*v.*)

Date: _____

2
assembled, Oliver Cromwell, abuse, practical, victory, bloody, inexperienced, forests, reward, trial, treason, sustain

- **assembled:** brought together parts or people (*v.*)
- **abuse:** the improper or hurtful use of something (*n.*)
- **practical:** straightforward and useful (*adj.*)
- **treason:** the crime of going against one's government (*n.*)
- **sustain:** to support with strength and guidance (*v.*)

Date: _____

3
society, happen, forced, government, opposed, yearned, unrest, lawmakers, title, protector

- **society:** a group of people who share a way of life (*n.*)
- **opposed:** acted against; stood in the way of (*v.*)
- **yearned:** hoped for; strongly wanted (*v.*)
- **protector:** a person who keeps someone or something from harm (*n.*)

Date: _____

4
long-exiled, traces, erased, restored, creation, parties, Tory, Whig, compromises, limited, threat

- **exiled:** forced from one's own country (*v.*)
- **traces:** small signs or marks left behind by someone or something (*n.*)
- **restored:** brought back to original condition (*v.*)
- **compromises:** agreements where both sides each get some, but not all, of what they want (*n.*)

Date: _____

5
festive, merry, younger, positions, tortured, impossible, consent

- **festive:** full of joy (*adj.*)
- **faith:** religion; set of beliefs (*n.*)
- **consent:** agreement (*n.*)

Date: _____

Mark this Flight on your timeline:

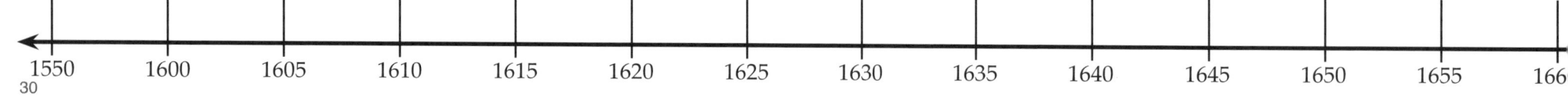

Post-Flight Debriefing

Date: _____

Flight 14: Charles & Cromwell

Use your imagery to answer questions for the whole Flight:

A. What is the main concept of this Flight?

_____
_____
_____

B. Who ordered the execution of King Charles I?

   a) the people of England
   b) Lord Oliver Cromwell
   c) his eldest son, Charles II
   d) none of the above

C. What religion did King James II want to convert England to?

   a) Islam
   b) Judaism
   c) Catholicism
   d) Buddhism

D. What lessons did England learn from being ruled by men who thought they were above the law?

_____
_____
_____

Charles I stood on a tall platform in the middle of the town square. His hands were tied behind his back. Suddenly, he…

_____
_____
_____
_____
_____
_____
_____
_____
_____
_____
_____
_____
_____
_____

Flight 15

Pre-Flight for The Sun King

Preread words for each paragraph:

Study and visualize the vocabulary:

1
foretell, parents, Austria, history, battles, distance, military, tactics, strategy, wider

Date: _____

foretell: to tell of something before it happens (v.)
tactics: techniques used to win in battle (n.)
strategy: the study of planning and directing battles (n.)
wider: extending beyond a given place (adj.)

2
declared, councils, adopted, symbol, Apollo, poems, Theresa, gala

Date: _____

right: a just claim to something (n.)
councils: groups of people who give advice (n.)
lavishly: done in a great amount, as though without limits (adv.)
gala: a happy celebration (n.)

3
massive, acres, gilded, ordered

Date: _____

massive: very large (adj.)
gilded: covered with a thin layer of gold (adj.)
court: the king's advisors and followers (n.)
stroll: to walk without purpose (v.)

4
followers, nicely, luxuries, enjoyed, concerts, gambling, everything

Date: _____

trail: a group that follows along behind someone (n.)
luxuries: things that give great comfort and pleasure, but are very expensive (n.)
vast: of great size or number (adj.)
gambling: betting money on the outcome of something (n.)

5
dreamed, costly, finery, heavily, outraged, peasants, protested, riots, shortly, realized, trouble, great-grandson, deathbed, absolute

Date: _____

finery: expensive clothes (n.)
peasants: poor farmers with low social standing (n.)
riots: violent outbursts in the streets, caused by crowds of people (n.)
fond: have a liking for (adj.)
absolute: completely; without limits or restrictions (adv.)

Mark this Flight on your timeline:

Post-Flight Debriefing

Date: _____

Flight 15: The Sun King

Use your imagery to answer questions for the whole Flight:

A. How would you summarize this Flight?

B. What symbol did King Louis XIV adopt?

  a) the sun
  b) a sword
  c) a royal crown
  d) the Bible

C. What did one lucky guest get to do each morning for Louis XIV?

  a) brush his teeth
  b) serve the King his breakfast
  c) sing him a song
  d) hand the King his royal shirt

D. How do you think the people of France felt when they saw the King lavishly spending all the money they paid in taxes?

One morning, Louis XIV was strolling the hallway of his palace when he crossed paths with a servant who was dressed in plain, ugly clothes. Outraged, Louis…

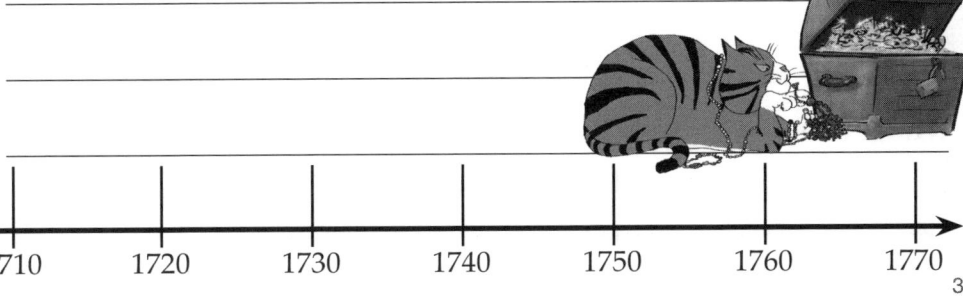

1665 1670 1675 1680 1685 1690 1700 1710 1720 1730 1740 1750 1760 1770

Flight 16

Pre-Flight for Isaac Newton

Preread words for each paragraph:

Study and visualize the vocabulary:

1
Isaac, marriage, whenever
Newton, stepfather, uncle
Christmas, farming, university
grandmother

shy: being nervous or unwilling to talk around other people (adj.)
marriage: the state of being married to another person (n.)
university: a school for higher learning where the highest degrees are awarded (n.)

Date: _____

2
handsome, learning, telescope
modest, experiments, happiest
Cambridge, prism, running
astronomy, mixture, intently
degree, rainbow, focused

modest: not having a high view of one's self; humble (adj.)
astronomy: the study of outer space, including the stars and planets (n.)
experiments: tests done to prove or discover something (n.)
prism: a triangle-shaped piece of cut glass that separates light into colors (n.)
woo: to try to win someone's love or affection (v.)

Date: _____

3
discovering, wonder, planets
gravity, floating, exact
legend, orbit, accurately

gravity: the natural force that pulls objects together, especially toward the earth (n.)
legend: a famous story from the past that is most likely not true (n.)
orbit: the circular path of one object around another, especially in space (n.)
accurately: correctly; without mistakes (adv.)
tides: the periods of the rising and falling of sea level at a given place (n.)

Date: _____

4
detailed, timid, admirers
sensitive, nervous, critics
publish, breakdown, criticism
findings, Mathematica

sensitive: easily affected or offended by others (adj.)
publish: to print one's writings on a large scale so that others can read them (v.)
timid: easily scared; lacking courage (adj.)
nervous breakdown: a sudden onset of severe emotional distress (n.)
stress: a state of mental pressure and tension (n.)

Date: _____

5
recovered, mercury, vital
service, poisoning, research
wavered

academic: related to study and teaching, as in a university (adj.)
knighted: given the title of knight, awarded for great merit (v.)
wavered: showed indecision between choices (v.)
mercury: a shiny metal that is a heavy liquid at room temperature (n.)
vital: being key to the life or existence of something (adj.)

Date: _____

Mark this Flight on your timeline:

1550 1600 1605 1610 1615 1620 1625 1630 1635 1640 1645 1650 1655 166

Post-Flight Debriefing

Date: _____

Flight 16: Isaac Newton

Use your imagery to answer questions for the whole Flight:

A. What is this Flight about?

B. What did Newton discover about light when he passed it through a prism?

   a) It turned clear light into a single bright red color.
   b) It split into a rainbow of colors.
   c) The prism absorbed the light and stopped it from shining through the other side.
   d) none of the above

C. Who used Newton's knowledge of gravity to measure ocean tides?

   a) fishermen
   b) surfers
   c) weathermen
   d) sailors

D. Do you think Newton's research affects our world today? Why or why not?

Newton tapped his foot nervously. The other scientists were shaking their heads. "I do not agree," one said. Insulted, Newton…

1665 1670 1675 1680 1685 1690 1700 1710 1720 1730 1740 1750 1760 1770

Flight 17 — Pre-Flight for The Explorers

Preread words for each paragraph:

Study and visualize the vocabulary:

1
- Jolliet
- explore
- adventure
- exploration
- trekked
- wild
- region
- knives
- beaver
- Mississippi
- empty
- Pacific

trekked: hiked or traveled slowly and with difficulty (v.)
beaver: an animal with soft brown fur and a wide flat tail that builds homes in ponds and rivers (n.)
pelts: the furs and skins of animals, often used in trading (n.)

Date: _____

2
- governor
- canoes
- supplies
- Jacques
- Marquette
- chosen
- paddle
- drained
- marvelled
- drifted
- waterway

governor: person in charge of leading and directing a region (n.)
canoes: long thin wooden boats moved with paddles (n.)
marvelled: expressed wonder and amazement at something or someone (v.)

Date: _____

3
- friendly
- hostile
- traders
- emptied
- journals
- rapids
- upset
- redraw
- memory
- record
- journey

hostile: unfriendly; hateful (adj.)
journals: daily written records of someone's thoughts or experiences (n.)
rapids: fast-moving part of a river with many rocks and swirling water (n.)
journey: a long trip (n.)

Date: _____

4
- Sieur De La Salle
- permission
- length
- Louisiana

fur trader: person who trades animal skins and fur for money and other goods (n.)
posts: stations in the wild where people can get supplies (n.)

Date: _____

5
- struck
- pirates
- raided
- swampy
- angry
- colonists

pirates: people on ships who attack other ships and steal from them (n.)
raided: attacked suddenly to steal things (v.)
mouth: the place where a stream or river runs into a large body of water, like the sea (n.)
swampy: wet and muddy, with many plants and creatures (adj.)

Date: _____

Mark this Flight on your timeline:

1550 | 1600 | 1605 | 1610 | 1615 | 1620 | 1625 | 1630 | 1635 | 1640 | 1645 | 1650 | 1655 | 166

Post-Flight Debriefing

Date: _____

Flight 17: The Explorers

Use your imagery to answer questions for the whole Flight:

A. What is the main idea for this Flight?

_____

_____

_____

B. What did *Mississippi* mean in the American Indian language?
  a) large canoe
  b) many rocks
  c) big river
  d) flooded land

C. Why did the explorers turn around instead of following the Mississippi River all the way to the Gulf of Mexico?
  a) Their canoes had leaks in them.
  b) The American Indians warned the explorers of hostile Spanish traders down the river.
  c) The French government sent word to have the explorers return home.
  d) They lost a battle with the American Indians in the area and were badly wounded.

D. Why do you think it was important to explore and map the Mississippi River?

_____

_____

Write a Picture Summary for this Flight.

Flight 18 — Pre-Flight for The Great Fire & Plague

Preread words for each paragraph:

Study and visualize the vocabulary:

1
- overcrowded
- taverns
- markets
- attracted
- butlers
- ditches
- common
- laborers
- narrow
- stench
- rummaged
- multiplying
- rapidly

stench: a strong, bad smell (n.)
rummaged: moved things around in search of something (v.)
multiplying: greatly increasing in number (v.)

Date: _____

2
- stifling
- breeding
- infested
- prisons
- neighborhoods
- nurses
- piled

stifling: lacking fresh or cool air, making it hard to breathe (adj.)
breeding: producing offspring (v.)
prisons: places where people who have broken the law are locked up (n.)
graves: holes dug in the ground to bury dead bodies (n.)

Date: _____

3
- returned
- London
- disaster
- baker's
- burst
- shoddy
- straw-covered
- consumed
- Thames

disaster: an event causing great destruction and upset (n.)
burst: to come forth all of a sudden and with great force (v.)
shoddy: cheaply or poorly made (n.)

Date: _____

4
- reported
- St. Paul's
- exploded
- lead
- desperate
- gunpowder
- debris
- exhausted
- Londoners
- destroyed
- thousands
- homeless

lead: a soft, heavy metal that is easily shaped (n.)
desperate: reckless, due to great need or panic (adj.)
debris: broken pieces and remains (n.)

Date: _____

5
- wasted
- rebuilding
- safer
- widened
- squads
- Wren
- emerged
- afterwards

squads: groups of people that work together for one task (n.)
emerged: came out of; appeared (v.)

Date: _____

Mark this Flight on your timeline:

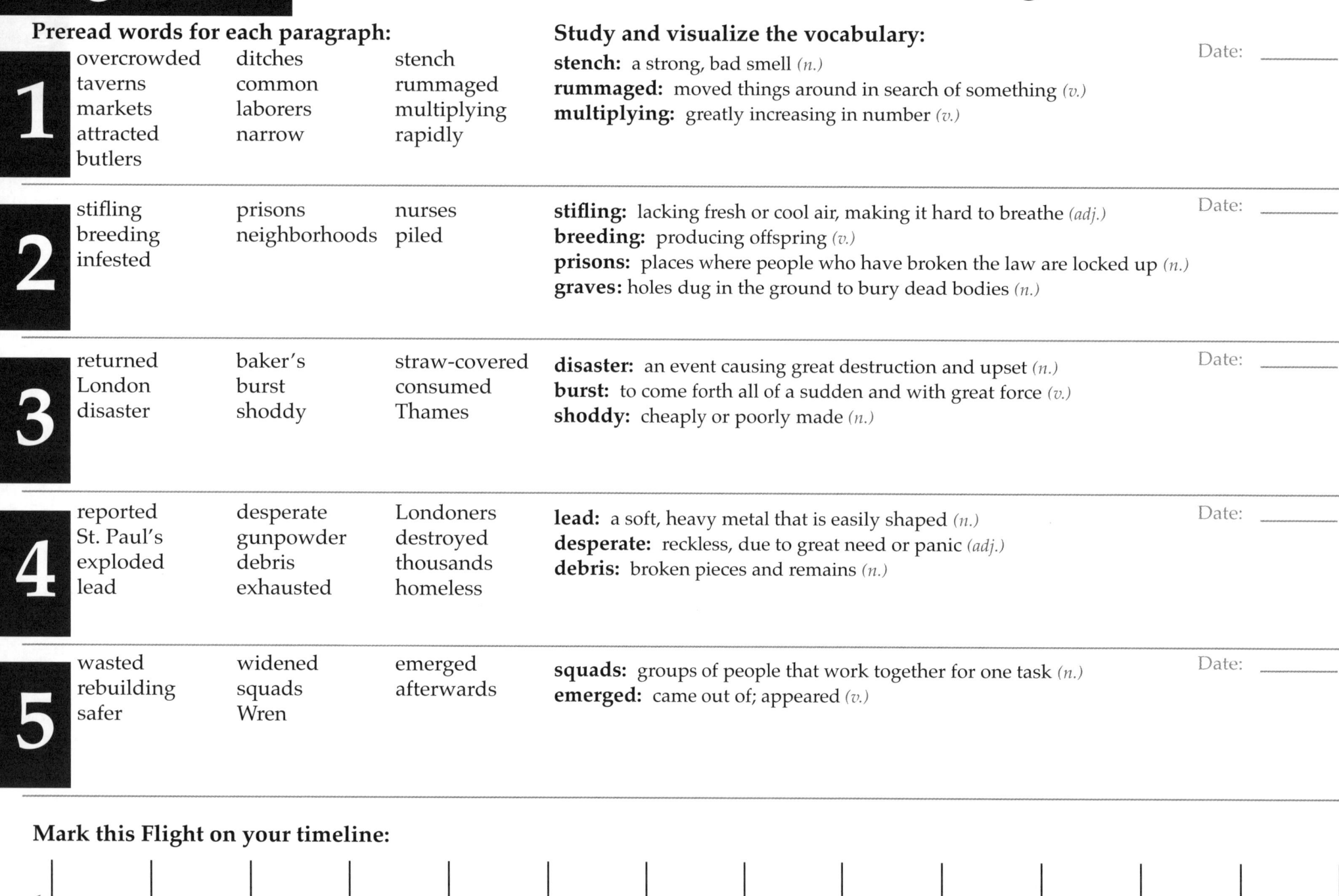

1550 | 1600 | 1605 | 1610 | 1615 | 1620 | 1625 | 1630 | 1635 | 1640 | 1645 | 1650 | 1655 | 1660

Post-Flight Debriefing

Date: _____

Flight 18: The Great Fire & Plague

Use your imagery to answer questions for the whole Flight:

A. What is the main concept of this Flight?

B. What was painted on the front door of a family's house if members of that family had the Plague?

   a) a yellow happy face
   b) a small blue circle
   c) a green star
   d) a large red cross

C. What started the Great Fire of London?

   a) Children were playing with fireworks inside a house.
   b) A baker's shop burst into flames.
   c) A campfire at a local gypsy camp got out of control.
   d) A man threw a lit cigar into a field.

D. Do you think London was a better or worse city to live in after the Great Fire? Explain.

The flames were getting close to the house. The family scrambled to get their things and get out in time. Suddenly, they heard a loud crash and…

Flight 19 — Pre-Flight for French and Indian Wars

Preread words for each paragraph:

Study and visualize the vocabulary:

1
clashed   horrified   themselves
tears   distant

clashed: disagreed violently (v.)
horrified: struck with great fear and disgust (v.)
distant: far off (adj.)

Date: _____

2
William   secretly   losses
longtime   allies   signed
owned   trudged

trudged: walked in a tired and difficult way (v.)
truce: an agreement to stop fighting (n.)

Date: _____

3
fragile   quiet   territory
Anne   Deerfield   Acadia
foggy   Port Royal   scuffled
attacked   relying   borders

fragile: easily broken (adj.)
relying: making great use of (v.)
territory: area of land (n.)
scuffled: fought or argued without serious injury (v.)
borders: outlines of a city, state, or country (n.)

Date: _____

4
Louisburg   George   surrendered
St. Lawrence   encircled   Ohio

encircled: surrounded (v.)
surrendered: gave up (v.)
guard: to protect (v.)
demanded: asked as though laying claim to a right (v.)
refused: determined not to give in or agree (v.)

Date: _____

5
Washington   defenses   safety
general   unexperienced   command
Braddock   horseback   Canada
Duquesne   bravely

defenses: obstacles that help protect against attack (n.)
bravely: facing danger with no sign of fear (adv.)
command: control and direction (n.)

Date: _____

Mark this Flight on your timeline:

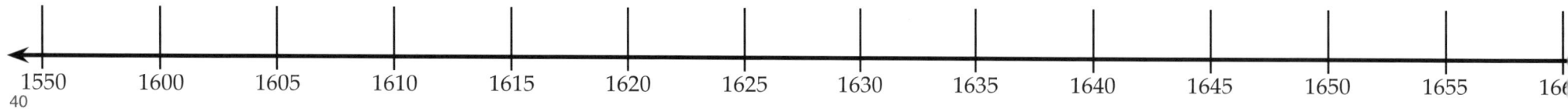

1550   1600   1605   1610   1615   1620   1625   1630   1635   1640   1645   1650   1655   1660

Post-Flight Debriefing

Date: _____

Flight 19: French and Indian Wars

Use your imagery to answer questions for the whole Flight:

A. How would you summarize this Flight?

_____

_____

_____

B. What important river near Fort Louisburg did the French want to prevent the English from using?

   a) St. Lawrence River
   b) Mississippi River
   c) Hudson River
   d) Columbia River

C. Why did the French win the battle of Duquesne?

   a) The English ran out of gunpowder for their weapons.
   b) The French were trained by the natives to use trees as defenses and the English general was inexperienced.
   c) The English grew tired of fighting and withdrew.
   d) all of the above

D. Why do you think the English and the French were such bitter enemies?

_____

_____

_____

With their muskets at the ready, General Braddock led his men slowly into the forest. The French hid quietly behind the trees until suddenly…

_____

_____

_____

_____

_____

_____

_____

_____

_____

_____

_____

_____

_____

_____

1665 1670 1675 1680 1685 1690 1700 1710 1720 1730 1740 1750 1760 1770

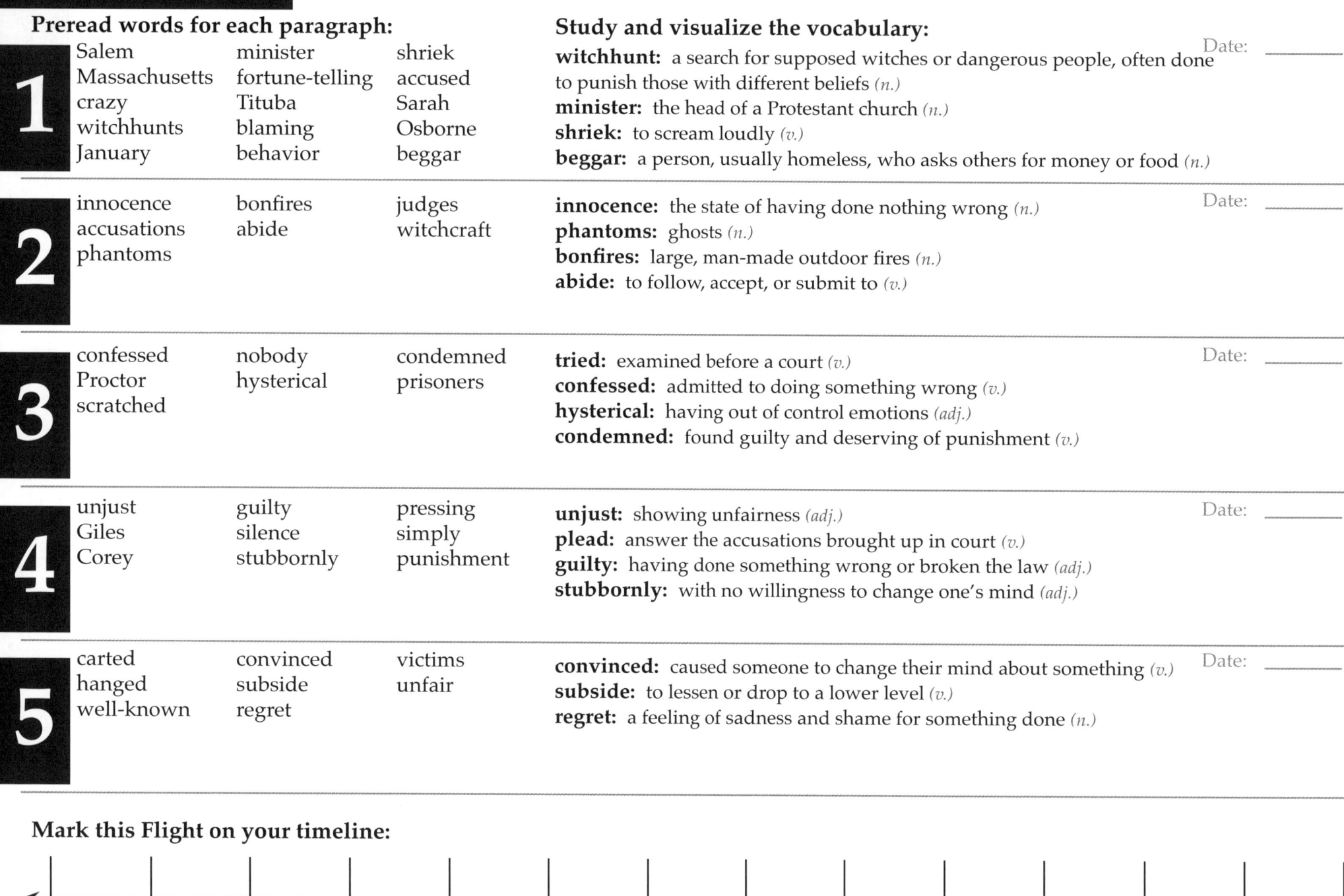

Post-Flight Debriefing

Date: _____

Flight 20: Salem Witch Trials

Use your imagery to answer questions for the whole Flight:

A. What is this Flight about?

_____
_____
_____

B. Who taught the young girls the fortune-telling tricks?

    a) John Proctor
    b) a Puritan minister
    c) Tituba
    d) Sarah Osborne

C. How did Giles Corey die?

    a) He was hung from a tree on a nearby hill.
    b) The town sheriff shot him.
    c) He starved to death in a prison cell.
    d) He was pressed to death under heavy rocks.

D. Why do you think it took so long for the witch trials and the wrongful accusations to end?

As the shy woman walked down the street in Salem, a young girl jumped out from behind a bush. "A witch!" the girl cried, pointing at the woman. Confused, the woman…

_____
_____
_____
_____
_____
_____
_____
_____
_____
_____
_____
_____
_____
_____
_____
_____

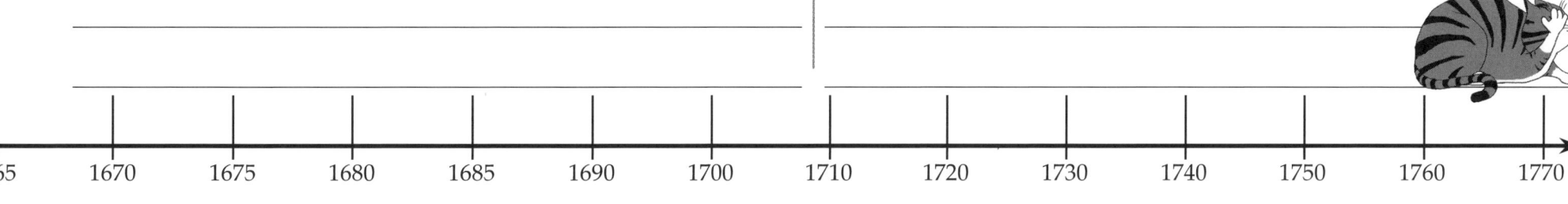

Flight 21 — Pre-Flight for Peter the Great

Preread words for each paragraph:

Study and visualize the vocabulary:

1
Romanov, half-sister, described
Russia, Sofia, isolated

Date: _____

crown prince: the prince that will inherit the throne from his parents (n.)
half-sister: a sister that shares only one parent (n.)
isolated: kept apart from (v.)
strong-willed: having great strength of mind to do something (adj.)

2
fascinated, loyal, firing
practice, shipbuilding, highly
naval, carpentry, czar
teenager, printing, dozens
recruited

Date: _____

fascinated: held one's attention; greatly interested someone (v.)
naval: having to do with warships and their sailors (adj.)
recruited: convinced someone to join something, especially a military unit (v.)
loyal: dedicated to someone or something (adj.)
carpentry: the work of building things out of wood (n.)

3
heir, reform, smartest
ignored, retrain, false
barracks

Date: _____

urging: insistence or encouragement (n.)
heir: someone who gets the position and property of a person when that person dies (n.)
barracks: a building that houses soldiers (n.)
reform: to form over again, usually to fix some problem (v.)
mills: factories that grind grain into flour, or cut trees into boards (n.)

4
modernize, teachers, defend
bribery, perform, radical
legal, actually, sweeping
staffed, duty, cheered

Date: _____

modernize: to bring up to date (v.)
legal system: the people, offices, and rules that control the way laws are enforced (n.)
duty: something a person is required to do (n.)
radical: very different; making great change (adj.)
sweeping: complete and thorough (adj.)

5
extreme, crafted, eldest
major, Russians, Alexei
exporting

Date: _____

extreme: very great; drastic (adj.)
exporting: sending goods out of the country they were made in, to sell them in another country (v.)
eldest: oldest (adj.)

Mark this Flight on your timeline:

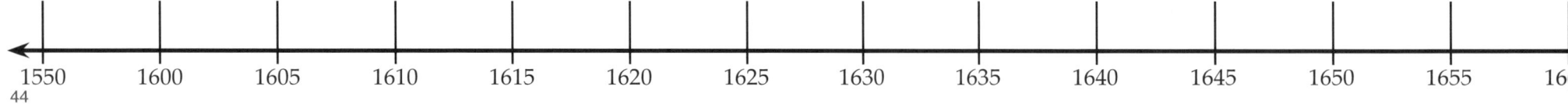

1550   1600   1605   1610   1615   1620   1625   1630   1635   1640   1645   1650   1655   16

44

Post-Flight Debriefing

Date: _____

Flight 21: Peter the Great

Use your imagery to answer questions for the whole Flight:

A. What is this Flight about?

_____

_____

_____

B. Which of these does NOT describe Peter the Great?

 a) He made the Russian men shave their beards.
 b) He read books and learned about other countries.
 c) He closed all of the colleges in Russia.
 d) He trained a group of soldiers when he was a teen.

C. Why did Peter the Great send Russian men to Europe?

 a) as punishment for crimes the men had done
 b) so they could learn new skills
 c) There was not enough food in Russia to feed everyone.
 d) so they could search for gold

D. Why was Peter the Great such an important figure in Russian history?

_____

_____

_____

_____

Based on your imagery, write a Picture Summary for this Flight.

_____

_____

_____

_____

_____

_____

_____

_____

_____

_____

_____

_____

_____

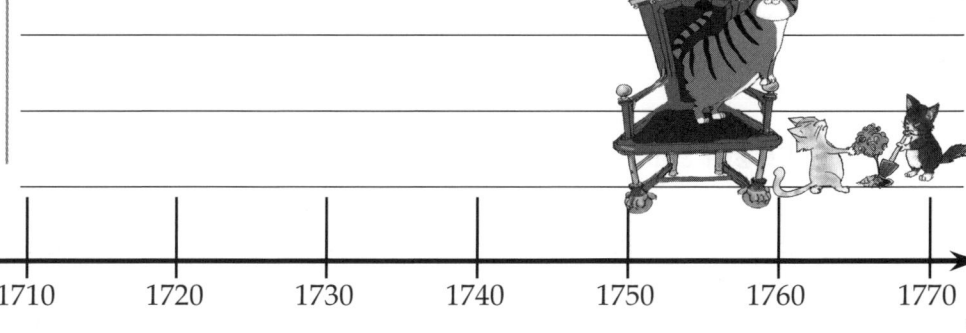

65	1670	1675	1680	1685	1690	1700	1710	1720	1730	1740	1750	1760	1770

Flight 22 — Pre-Flight for Vivaldi

Preread words for each paragraph:

Study and visualize the vocabulary:

1
Antonio Vivaldi, Venice, acclaimed, musician, violinist, red-headed, ordained, orphanage

Date: _____

acclaimed: greatly praised by the audiences and critics *(adj.)*
violinist: someone who plays the violin *(n.)*
Mass: a Catholic church service held every week *(n.)*
ordained: made someone a priest or minister *(v.)*
orphanage: a place that houses and cares for children with no parents *(n.)*

2
complain, tightness, breathe, excuse, composing, pieces, orchestra

Date: _____

preach: to talk to people about religion *(n.)*
orchestra: a group of people who play music together, with many different instruments *(n.)*
screen: a thin structure used to divide or block a space *(n.)*

3
engraved, concertos, popular, mimicked, together

Date: _____

concertos: pieces of music in which a single instrument plays, and is backed up by an orchestra *(n.)*
rare: not normally seen; special *(adj.)*
flute: an instrument shaped like a long, thin tube that makes soft, high-pitched sounds *(n.)*
mimicked: imitated; copied *(v.)*

4
seasons, chirping, scorches, crackling, grasses, gnats, clacking, chatter

Date: _____

scorches: burns or dries up *(v.)*
gnats: tiny flying insects *(n.)*
sound: to make a sound as a call *(v.)*
roar: a loud rumbling or rushing sound *(n.)*
clacking: the sharp sound of two hard things hitting together *(adj.)*

5
directed, actors, resigned, unmarked, sadly, forgotten

Date: _____

managed: took charge and care of *(v.)*
resigned: gave up and left one's job *(v.)*

Mark this Flight on your timeline:

Post-Flight Debriefing

Date: _____

Flight 22: Vivaldi

Use your imagery to answer questions for the whole Flight:

A. What is the main idea for this Flight?

_____

_____

_____

B. What is the name of Vivaldi's most famous musical work?

   a) *Dreamcatcher*
   b) *The Gardener*
   c) *The Four Seasons*
   d) *Circus Animals*

C. Which of these describes Vivaldi?

   a) He had his music engraved on metal plates.
   b) He wrote music for an all-girls orchestra.
   c) He liked to single out an instrument to mimic natural sounds.
   d) all of the above

D. Why might audiences be interested in Vivaldi's music?

_____

_____

_____

The orchestra began to play Vivaldi's new piece of music. The sounds of the instruments made the audience picture…

_____

_____

_____

_____

_____

_____

_____

_____

_____

_____

_____

_____

_____

_____

| 1665 | 1670 | 1675 | 1680 | 1685 | 1690 | 1700 | 1710 | 1720 | 1730 | 1740 | 1750 | 1760 | 1770 |

Flight 23

Pre-Flight for J.S. Bach

Preread words for each paragraph:

Study and visualize the vocabulary:

1
Johann Sebastian Bach, earmarked, success, organist, repair, valves, tighten, tiptoed, cabinet, favorite, copied

- **earmarked:** chosen for a specific purpose (v.)
- **organs:** instruments with keyboards that play compressed air through pipes (n.)
- **valves:** devices that vary the amount of air passing through a tube (n.)
- **cabinet:** a piece of furniture with shelves and drawers (n.)

Date: _____

2
Latin, exchange, scolded, another

- **exchange:** a trade (n.)
- **skipped:** avoided; did not attend (v.)
- **scolded:** talked angrily at someone for doing something wrong (v.)

Date: _____

3
Barbara, children, Weimar, pedals, mighty, equally, precision

- **duke:** the ruler of a small state, especially in Europe (n.)
- **mighty:** powerful (adj.)
- **equally:** in the same manner (adv.)
- **precision:** the state of being exact and correct (n.)

Date: _____

4
Leopold, Cothen, director, illness, grieving, singer, Leipzig, arguing

- **sudden:** unexpected; rapidly setting in (adj.)
- **grieving:** feeling deep sadness and pain over the loss of someone or something (v.)

Date: _____

5
eyesight, operations, heartbroken, blindness

- **operations:** surgeries (n.)
- **heartbroken:** very unhappy and hurt (adj.)
- **stroke:** the lodging of a blood clot in the brain, often causing loss of sight, speech, and movement (n.)

Date: _____

Mark this Flight on your timeline:

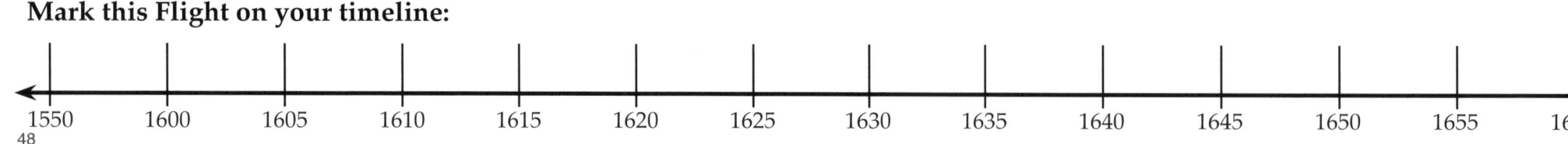

1550 1600 1605 1610 1615 1620 1625 1630 1635 1640 1645 1650 1655 16

Post-Flight Debriefing

Date: _____

Flight 23: J.S. Bach

Use your imagery to answer questions for the whole Flight:

A. What is the main idea for this Flight?

B. What musical instrument did Bach specialize in?

    a) violin
    b) organ
    c) trumpet
    d) piano

C. Which of these describes J.S. Bach?

    a) He invited guests to his home and played for them.
    b) He did not know how to fix organs.
    c) He worked at a butcher shop when he was a teen.
    d) He had no fans of his music until after his death.

D. What part of Bach's life is most interesting to you?

Write a Word Summary for J.S. Bach.

1665   1670   1675   1680   1685   1690   1700   1710   1720   1730   1740   1750   1760   1770

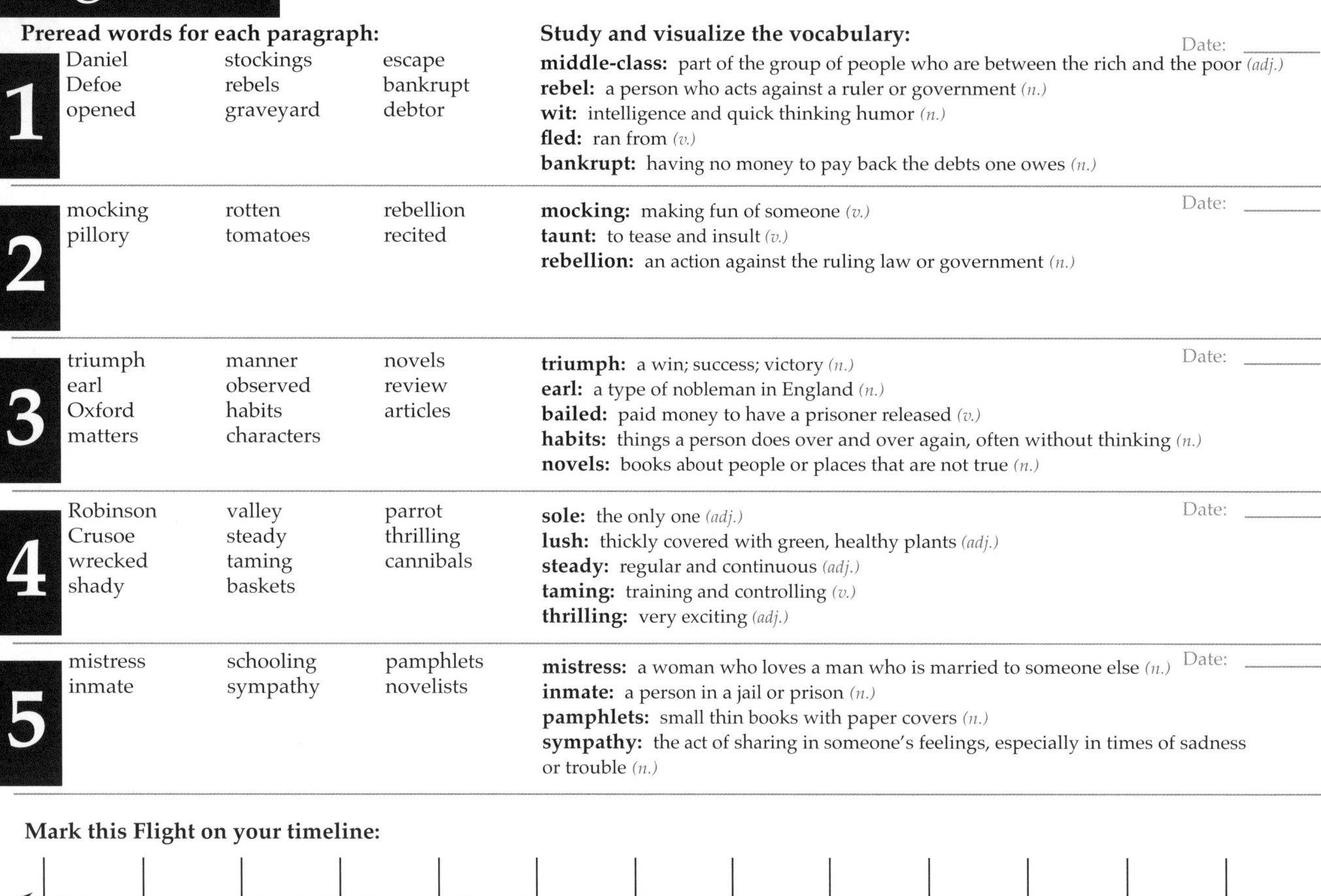

Post-Flight Debriefing

Date: _____

Flight 24: Daniel Defoe

Use your imagery to answer questions for the whole Flight:

A. What is this Flight about?

_____
_____
_____

B. What is Defoe's novel *Robinson Crusoe* about?

    a) a peasant who becomes a king
    b) a man who spent nearly his entire life in jail
    c) a man who learns how to live alone on an island
    d) a sea voyage around the world

C. Which of these did NOT happen to Daniel Defoe?

    a) He was locked in a pillory.
    b) He founded and wrote his own newspaper.
    c) He was praised by the Church of England.
    d) He was bailed out of jail and hired by an Earl.

D. How might Defoe's life experiences have helped him write great novels?

_____
_____
_____

Defoe was locked in the pillory in front of a huge crowd. As the crowd began to tease him, he…

_____
_____
_____
_____
_____
_____
_____
_____
_____
_____
_____
_____
_____
_____

1665 1670 1675 1680 1685 1690 1700 1710 1720 1730 1740 1750 1760 1770

Flight 25
Pre-Flight for Jonathan Swift

Preread words for each paragraph:

Study and visualize the vocabulary:

1
- Jonathan
- Swift
- Dublin
- Ireland
- fantasy
- boarding
- trinity
- conceited
- relative
- poetry
- satire
- Esther
- Johnson
- fondly
- Stella

fantasy: imaginary; not real (adj.)
boarding school: a school where students live and study, often far from their homes (n.)
conceited: thinking very highly of oneself (adj.)
relative: a member of one's family (n.)
satire: writing that makes fun of people or events in order to make people laugh (n.)

Date: _____

2
- Moor
- parish
- bothered
- cruelly
- Irish
- lower
- witty
- St. Patrick
- solitary

parish: a small area that has its own church and pastor (n.)
bothered: upset or annoyed (v.)
dean: a person who is the head of a school or department (n.)
solitary: alone (adj.)

Date: _____

3
- stinging
- Gulliver
- Lemuel
- represents
- shipwrecked
- sunbeams
- cucumbers
- barely
- normal
- voyage
- stupid
- Yahoos

stinging: causing irritation or emotional pain (adj.)
trait: a feature that someone or something is known for (n.)
sunbeams: rays of light from the sun (n.)
voyage: a long trip; journey (n.)
airs: habits and manners that are silly or insincere (n.)

Date: _____

4
- proposal
- landlords
- suggested
- hungry
- wholesome
- whether
- treatment
- heartless
- sickened

proposal: a plan or offer (n.)
wholesome: healthy (adj.)
stewed: cooked for a long time in hot liquid (v.)
broiled: cooked by putting very close to a flame (v.)

Date: _____

5
- lonely
- undiagnosed
- nauseous
- dizzy
- sanity
- hospital
- insane
- notoriety
- revered
- national
- homeland
- mourned

undiagnosed: unknown or unidentified (adj.)
nauseous: sick to one's stomach, often causing one to throw up (adj.)
sanity: the state of having a healthy mind (n.)
notoriety: state of being known by many, usually for something bad (n.)
revered: admired and respected (v.)

Date: _____

Mark this Flight on your timeline:

1550 1600 1605 1610 1615 1620 1625 1630 1635 1640 1645 1650 1655 16

Post-Flight Debriefing

Date: _____

Flight 25: Jonathan Swift

Use your imagery to answer questions for the whole Flight:

A. What is the main idea for this Flight?

_____

_____

_____

B. Which of these is NOT a land Gulliver visits in Swift's *Gulliver's Travels*?

a) a land ruled by grasshoppers
b) a land of mad scientists
c) a land of giants
d) a land of talking horses

C. What inspired Swift to write his bitter pamphlet, *A Modest Proposal*?

a) He observed the English cruelly treating the Irish.
b) the memory of his difficult childhood
c) All of Swift's belongings were stolen.
d) the love he felt for his longtime friend Stella

D. Why do you think Swift used satire in his writing?

_____

_____

_____

Lemuel Gulliver set sail and arrived at a land of giants. As he stepped ashore…

_____

_____

_____

_____

_____

_____

_____

_____

_____

_____

_____

_____

_____

_____

_____

_____

1665 1670 1675 1680 1685 1690 1700 1710 1720 1730 1740 1750 1760 1770

Flight 26 — Pre-Flight for Frederick the Great

Preread words for each paragraph: **Study and visualize the vocabulary:**

1
Frederick, Prussia, disapproving, promised, daily, drilling

- **strict:** having many harsh rules *(adj.)*
- **crude:** rough; lacking good manners *(adj.)*
- **native:** coming from his own country *(adj.)*
- **disapproving:** not liking someone or something *(adj.)*
- **aim:** to point a weapon *(v.)*

Date: _____

2
watchful, relaxing, discussed, carefree

- **watchful:** always looking out for something *(adj.)*
- **relaxing:** making one feel calm and peaceful *(adj.)*
- **carefree:** without worry *(adj.)*

Date: _____

3
teachings, Silesia, archduchess, invaded, hardly, Breslau, potatoes

- **proved:** showed something to be true, especially by acting *(v.)*
- **archduchess:** the wife of an archduke, who was the son of an emperor in Austria *(n.)*
- **invaded:** entered by force *(v.)*
- **coal:** a mineral dug from the ground and burned as fuel *(n.)*

Date: _____

4
unmatched, Saxony, series, courageous

- **unmatched:** having no equal *(adj.)*
- **series:** a group of things in a row that are related to each other *(n.)*
- **courageous:** very brave *(adj.)*

Date: _____

5
resolved, canals, combined, loveless, nephew, succeeded

- **resolved:** strongly decided *(v.)*
- **canals:** man-made paths dug out for water and boats to pass through *(n.)*
- **steel:** a strong metal made of carbon and iron, used for weapons and building *(n.)*

Date: _____

Mark this Flight on your timeline:

1550 | 1600 | 1605 | 1610 | 1615 | 1620 | 1625 | 1630 | 1635 | 1640 | 1645 | 1650 | 1655 | 16—

Post-Flight Debriefing

Date: _____

Flight 26: Frederick the Great

Use your imagery to answer questions for the whole Flight:

A. What is the main idea for this Flight?

_____
_____
_____

B. Which of these best describes Frederick the Great?

  a) He loved his wife very much, and paid a lot of attention to her.
  b) He hated reading, writing, theater, and music.
  c) He was a weak military leader.
  d) He was the king of Austria.

C. What did Frederick the Great do to make his country stronger?

  a) He created more farmland, and built better roads and canals.
  b) He built tall walls around his country so no one could leave or enter.
  c) He taught his soldiers to speak six different languages.
  d) all of the above

D. Do you think Frederick the Great's strict childhood helped him be a better king? Explain.

_____
_____

Write a Word Summary for Frederick the Great.

_____
_____
_____
_____
_____
_____
_____
_____
_____
_____
_____
_____

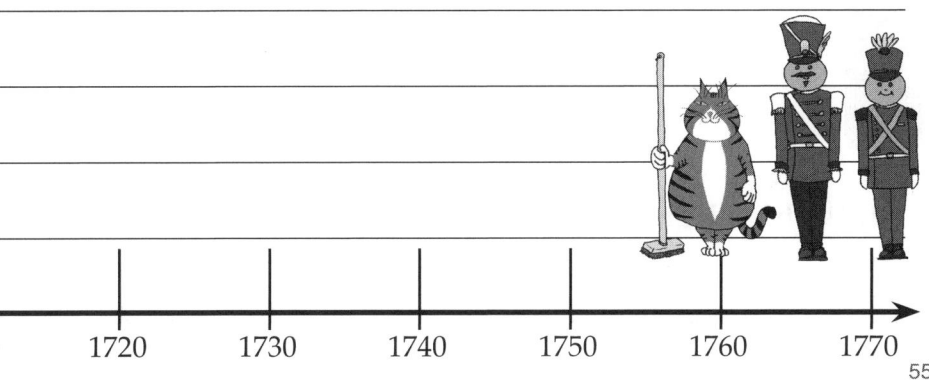

|1665 | 1670 | 1675 | 1680 | 1685 | 1690 | 1700 | 1710 | 1720 | 1730 | 1740 | 1750 | 1760 | 1770|

Flight 27

Pre-Flight for Maria Theresa

Preread words for each paragraph:

Study and visualize the vocabulary:

1
Vienna, issued, decree, emperor, shocking, decision, Habsburg

issued: gave; delivered *(v.)*
shocking: extremely surprising *(adj.)*
decree: an order given by a person in power *(n.)*

Date: _____

2
intelligence, bordered, cheerful

cheerful: happy; with good spirit *(adj.)*
spotlight: the center of others' attention *(n.)*
poise: a way of acting that is calm and self-confident *(n.)*

Date: _____

3
Francis, birthright, invasion, Stephen, determined, Bavaria, expected

wed: married *(v.)*
birthright: a privilege someone gained as soon as they were born *(n.)*
proud: to feel pleased about one's own efforts or skills *(adj.)*
character: personality *(n.)*
determined: decided and set out to do something *(v.)*

Date: _____

4
valuable, academy, accepted, empress, educate

valuable: having much worth *(adj.)*
elected: voted into some role by a group of people *(v.)*
military: having to do with soldiers and fighting *(adj.)*
academy: a school for special study *(n.)*

Date: _____

5
somewhat, glorious

dense: having a slow mind; not intelligent *(adj.)*
glorious: wonderful and full of honor *(adj.)*

Date: _____

Mark this Flight on your timeline:

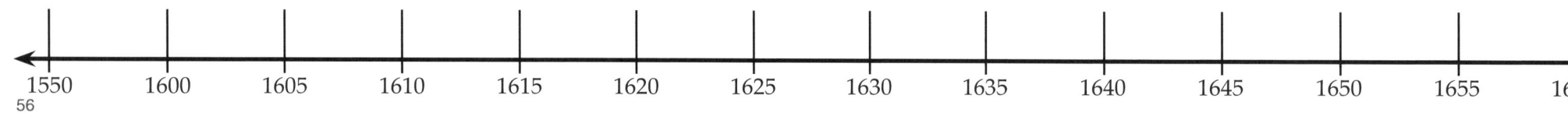

Post-Flight Debriefing

Date: _____

Use your imagery to answer questions for the whole Flight:

A. How would you summarize this Flight?

_____

_____

_____

B. Which of these does NOT describe Maria Theresa?

  a) She had a weak mind.
  b) She was kind and cheerful.
  c) She became an empress.
  d) She was not well trained as a leader before her father's death.

C. What did Maria Theresa do to build a stronger army?

  a) She hired Frederick the Great, of Prussia, to train her soldiers.
  b) She bribed men to join the army.
  c) She opened a military academy.
  d) She bought guns and cannons from China.

D. Considering all that you have pictured here, why do you think Maria Theresa was a rare woman for her time?

_____

_____

_____

Young Maria Theresa woke up from a good night's sleep and felt ready to face the day. As she walked through the palace...

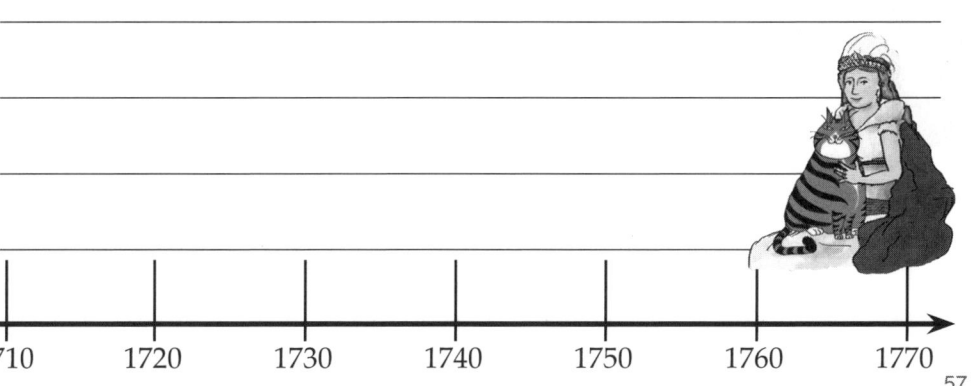

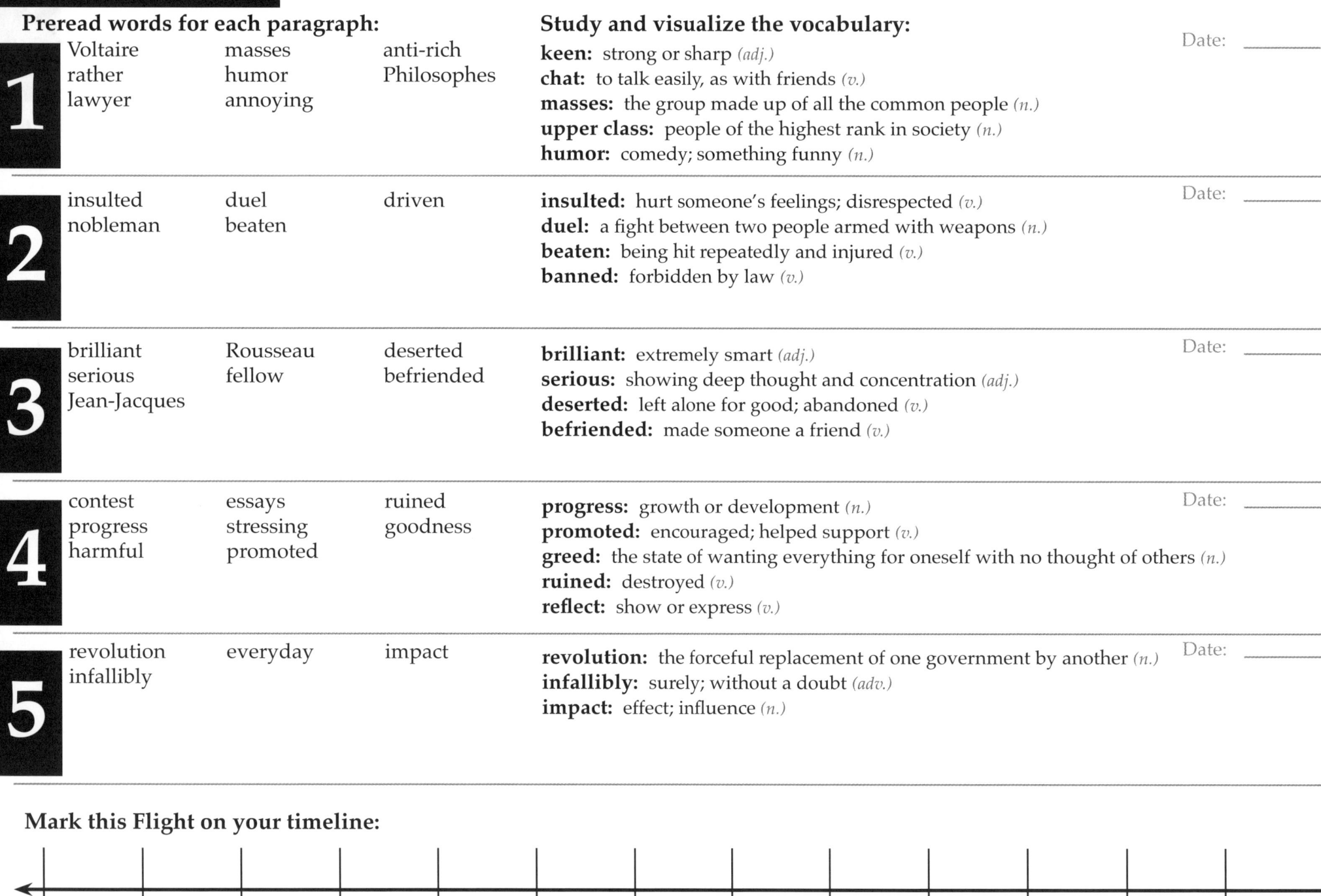

Post-Flight Debriefing

Date: _____

Flight 28: The Philosophes

Use your imagery to answer questions for the whole Flight:

A. What is this Flight about?

_____
_____
_____

B. Who were the Philosophes?
- a) a group of soap makers
- b) a group of thinkers with new ideas
- c) ex-convicts
- d) members of the French royal family

C. Which of these best describes the ideas expressed in Voltaire's and Rousseau's writings?
- a) French families should only be allowed to have two children.
- b) The poor should think for themselves, and should no longer be ruled by the rich.
- c) The wealthy men of France should be the only ones allowed to write laws.
- d) All books should be banned in Europe.

D. How do you think Voltaire and Rousseau helped the French people?

_____
_____
_____

Voltaire and Rousseau met other members of the Philosophes at a party. They all gathered in a circle and…

_____
_____
_____
_____
_____
_____
_____
_____
_____
_____
_____
_____
_____
_____

Flight 29 — Pre-Flight for Mozart

Preread words for each paragraph:

Study and visualize the vocabulary:

1
Wolfgang   prodigy   curly-haired
Amadeus   archbishop   dangling
Mozart   keyboard   squiggly

Date: _____

prodigy: a genius, especially one that is very young, with amazing abilities *(n.)*
keyboard: the row of keys of an instrument like a piano *(n.)*
dangling: hanging down and swinging *(v.)*
squiggly: having many curves and twists *(adj.)*

2
special   crawled   amazingly
outside

Date: _____

special: better or more unique than what is normal *(adj.)*
concerts: musical performances *(n.)*
crawled: to move slowly along the ground on hands and knees *(v.)*

3
giggly   symphony   image
astonished   outgrown   touring

Date: _____

giggly: full of silliness and laughter *(adj.)*
astonished: very amazed; greatly surprised *(v.)*
tours: trips made from place to place to do something *(n.)*
symphony: a long piece of music played by a full orchestra *(n.)*

4
premiered   disappear   absent
impulsive   notice   earning

Date: _____

premiered: showed or performed for the first time *(v.)*
impulsive: doing something suddenly and without thought *(adj.)*
absent: gone; not present *(adj.)*

5
Constanze   income   funeral
Weber   foolish   confined
selling   requiem

Date: _____

income: money earned by someone, from working, or given to them *(n.)*
foolish: not wise; stupid *(adj.)*
requiem: a piece of music played at a funeral *(n.)*

Mark this Flight on your timeline:

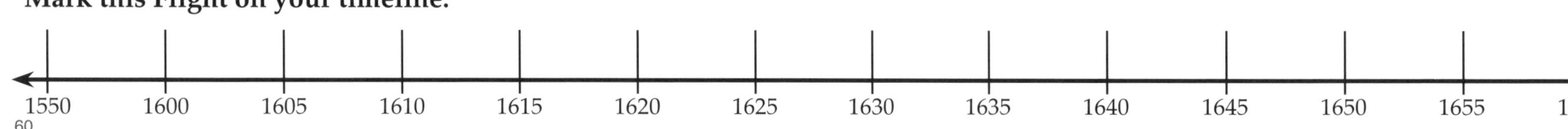

1550 1600 1605 1610 1615 1620 1625 1630 1635 1640 1645 1650 1655 16

Post-Flight Debriefing

Date: _____

Flight 29: Mozart

Use your imagery to answer questions for the whole Flight:

A. How would you summarize this Flight?

_____

_____

_____

B. How old was Mozart when he became a composer?

- a) thirty-five
- b) twelve
- c) five
- d) twenty-five

C. What was the last musical piece Mozart worked on before his death?

- a) a concerto
- b) a requiem
- c) a symphony
- d) an opera

D. Why do you think Mozart was an important figure in history?

_____

_____

A large crowd gathered to hear young Wolfgang play the keyboard. The small genius sat on a bench and...

_____

_____

_____

_____

_____

_____

_____

_____

_____

_____

_____

_____

_____

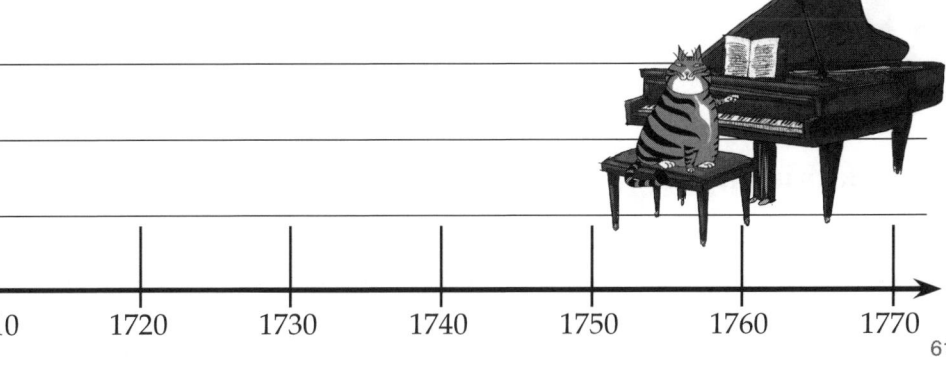

| 1665 | 1670 | 1675 | 1680 | 1685 | 1690 | 1700 | 1710 | 1720 | 1730 | 1740 | 1750 | 1760 | 1770 |

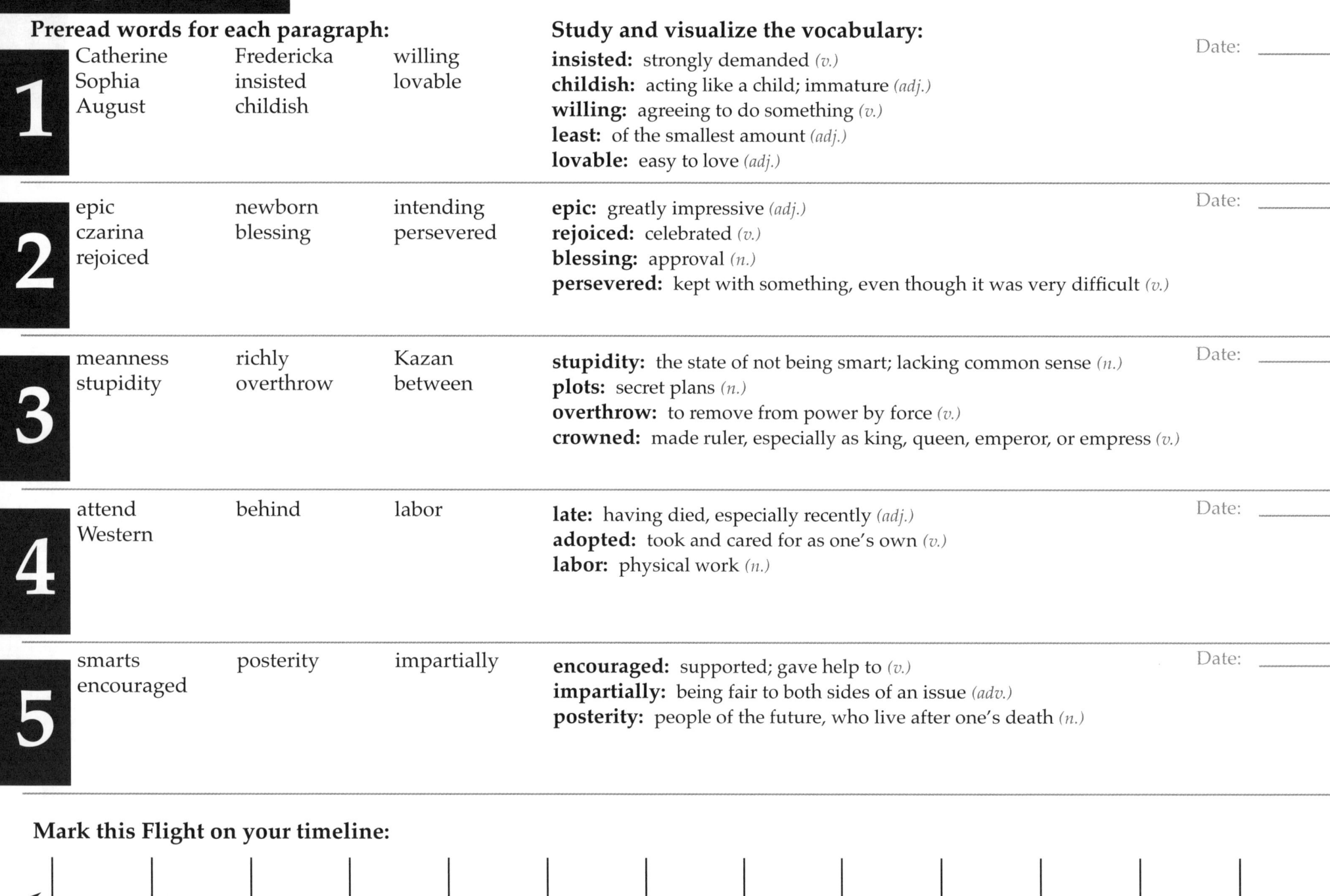

Post-Flight Debriefing

Date: _____

Use your imagery to answer questions for the whole Flight:

A. What is the main idea for this Flight?

_____

_____

_____

B. Why was Catherine the Great considered a great ruler?

   a) She increased Russia's trade.
   b) She set up schools and hospitals.
   c) She loved Russia's people and their country's history.
   d) all of the above

C. Why did Catherine the Great want to take the throne from her husband?

   a) Her husband made her dress all in black.
   b) Her husband was a weak ruler who taxed his people.
   c) Her husband put her under house arrest for 30 years.
   d) Her husband planned to attack her home country of Germany.

D. Do you think Catherine the Great was a better ruler than her husband, Czar Peter III? Why or why not?

_____

_____

Write a Word Summary for Catherine the Great.

Flight 30: Catherine the Great

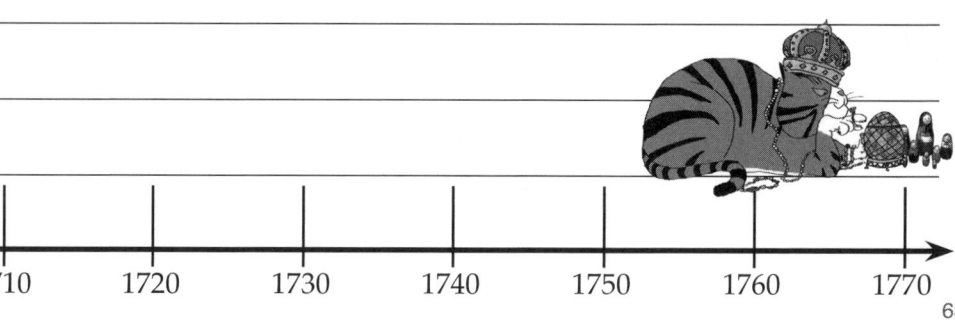

1665 1670 1675 1680 1685 1690 1700 1710 1720 1730 1740 1750 1760 1770

Flight 31 — Pre-Flight for James Cook

Preread words for each paragraph:

Study and visualize the vocabulary:

1
excelled harbor shippers
coastal seaport

Date: _____

excelled: did very well, better than others *(v.)*
coastal: found next to the ocean *(adj.)*
harbor: a protected part of a body of water where ships can dock *(n.)*
docks: platforms that stick out over the water for ships to pull up next to *(n.)*
longed: wished strongly *(v.)*

2
navigate scurvy charting
Endeavor healthy Venus
mission Tahiti

Date: _____

navigate: to plan the route for a trip *(v.)*
chart: maps made for ships and sailors *(n.)*
mission: an important task that must be done *(n.)*
scurvy: a deadly disease, once common among sailors, caused by lack of Vitamin C *(n.)*

3
paradise Australia overboard
New Zealand coral damage
rugged

Date: _____

paradise: a place of great beauty and joy *(n.)*
rugged: rocky, rough, and uneven *(adj.)*
coral: a growth of rough, rock-like skeletons of tiny marine animals *(n.)*
reef: a long ridge of rock, sand, or coral, just below the surface of the ocean *(n.)*

4
continent Antarctic samples
exist steering notebooks

Date: _____

continent: a large land mass *(n.)*
exist: to be present *(v.)*
steering: changing something's direction of movement *(v.)*

5
beaches Hawaii hostage
anchored

Date: _____

steep: tall and sharply sloping *(adj.)*
anchored: prevented a ship from moving by fixing an anchor to the seafloor *(v.)*
hostage: a person held unwillingly *(n.)*

Mark this Flight on your timeline:

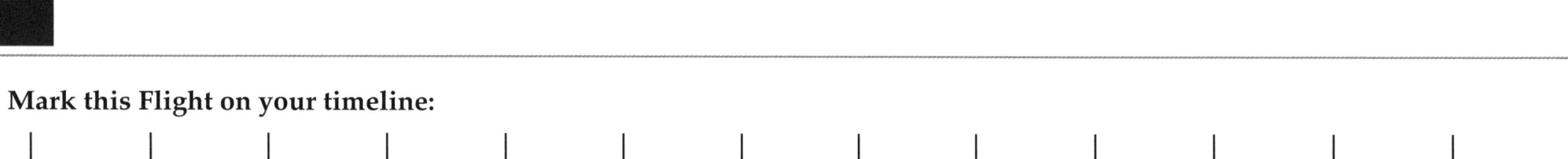

64

Post-Flight Debriefing

Date: _____

Use your imagery to answer questions for the whole Flight:

A. What is the main idea for this Flight?

_____
_____
_____

B. As captain of the *Endeavor*, what was Cook's mission?

a) to sail around the world in five days or less
b) to look for English sailors who were being held captive
c) to search for new lands that England could claim
d) to sail to China and trade leather for spices

C. Which of these was NOT a place Cook visited on one of his many voyages?

a) New Zealand
b) Greenland
c) Australia
d) Hawaii

D. Do you think the people of England considered Cook a hero? Why or why not?

_____
_____

Cook and his crew anchored their ship near the rugged coast of a tropical island. Once they rowed small boats ashore, they saw…

_____
_____
_____
_____
_____
_____
_____
_____
_____
_____
_____
_____
_____
_____

Flight 31: James Cook

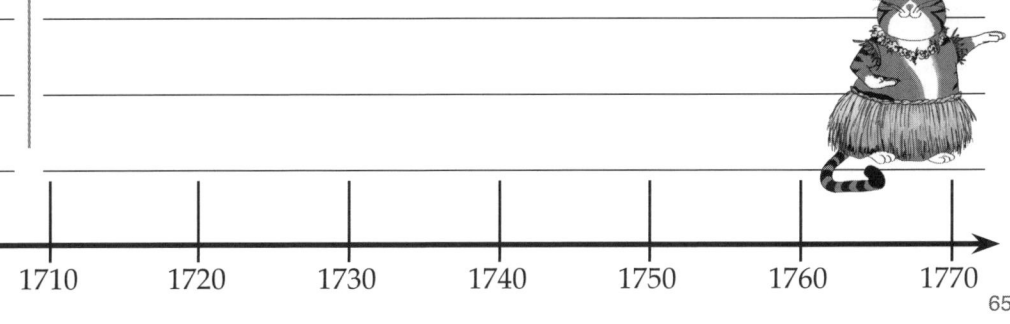

Notes

Analysis of Student Performance:

Notes

Analysis of Student Performance:

Notes

Analysis of Student Performance: